MAE WEST
BROADCAST MUSE

By

Michael Gregg Michaud

Some of the lyrics from these songs appear in the book. Copyright remains with the talented musicians and lyricists who composed these classic songs.

"I Wanna Go Home (With You)" Words and Music by Jack Joyce and Joe Candullo. 1949

"I'm In the Mood For Love" Words and Music by Dorothy Fields and Jimmy McHugh. 1935

"It's So Nice to Have A Man Around the House" Words and Music by Jack Elliott and Harold Spina. 1950

"Personality" Words and Music by Johnny Burke and Jimmy Van Heusen. 1946

"I Can't Give You Anything But Love, Baby" Words and Music by Dorothy Fields and Jimmy McHugh. 1928

MAE WEST: Broadcast Muse
© 2019. Michael Gregg Michaud. All rights reserved.

All illustrations are copyright of their respective owners, and are also reproduced here in the spirit of publicity. Whilst we have made every effort to acknowledge specific credits whenever possible, we apologize for any omissions, and will undertake every effort to make any appropriate changes in future editions of this book if necessary.

No part of this book may be reproduced in any form or by any means, electronic, mechanical, digital, photocopying or recording, except for the inclusion in a review, without permission in writing from the publisher.

Published in the USA by:
BearManor Media
P O Box 71426
Albany, Georgia 31708
www.bearmanormedia.com

Printed in the United States of America
ISBN   978-1-62933-438-7 (paperback)
           978-1-62933-439-4 (hardcover)

Book and cover design by Darlene Swanson • www.van-garde.com

"I never liked the idea of doing television because people could turn me off."

— Mae West to Joyce Haber, 1968

Mae West and Charlie McCarthy, 1937.

Contents

	A Nod to the Often Unsung Writers	vii
Chapter 1	*The Rudy Vallee Hour and The Chase and Sanborn Hour*	1
Chapter 2	*Mail Call*	31
Chapter 3	*The Chesterfield Supper Club*	41
Chapter 4	*It Ain't History, It's Herstory*	65
Chapter 5	Mae West Meets Oscar, and *The Mae West Show*	95
Chapter 6	Mae West Meets Dean Martin and Bob Hope	145
Chapter 7	*Person to Person*. On Again, Off Again	163
Chapter 8	Mae West Meets Cauliflower McPugg, San Fernando Red, and Clem Kadiddlehopper	169
Chapter 9	Mae West and a Talking Horse	191
Chapter 10	Armed Forces Radio Christmas Show	231
Chapter 11	*Dick Cavett's Backlot USA*	239
Chapter 12	The First Time, and the Last Time	253

Mae West and Red Skelton, 1960.

A Nod to the Often Unsung Writers

WRITING RADIO AND TELEVISION shows involved the collective effort of numerous writers. Sometimes a program employed a supervising, or "head," writer, but a staff of writers was involved with each script. Intern writers often contributed, and it was not uncommon that some of the writers did not get individual credit for their work. Some of these talented folks later moved on to individual success. Great respect is due to the many gifted writers, many of whom worked under pressure to complete scripts on a weekly, bi-weekly, and sometimes daily basis. Sometimes writers worked on the lines throughout the rehearsals, and even in the minutes leading up to the recording or live broadcast of the program. Trying to please the sponsor, the director, the producer, the stars, and the censors, was an arduous challenge.

 The sketches included here are presented as historical broadcast pieces, presented so the talents involved are not forgotten (even though most remain nameless), and their comedic talents can still be enjoyed. If the writers' names are known, they are properly and deservedly credited. Mae often claimed the writer credit for her few radio and television appearances. She may have tinkered with lines, but she was not responsible for the entire approved scripts. No such guarantee could be promised by broadcasters at that time, which is one of the reasons the actress rarely appeared on television.

I do not imply any ownership interest in the sketches and other scripted pieces. These works are not available for production or re-enactment without the express written permission of any current copyright holders. However, all the works included here are available to the public on LPs, CDs, DVDs, audio tapes, and freely on the internet.

The photos included here are from the personal collection of the author. The photographs enrich the text and are presented for historical purposes only. Any right to reproduce and market any images is strictly forbidden by law without the written permission of any copyright owners.

CHAPTER 1

The Rudy Vallee Hour and *The Chase and Sanborn Hour*

"Well, all I got to say is,
where there's smoke, there's fire."

Mae reviews the script for her first national radio broadcast on
The Rudy Vallee Hour.

MAE WEST WAS ALREADY riding a tidal wave of fame with the impending release of her soon to be Oscar-nominated film, *She Done Him Wrong*, on February 9, 1933. She traveled to New York to promote the film's Manhattan premiere and performed in a live stage show before evening screenings at the Paramount Theater. Fans stood in blocks-long lines to see the star, but critics were dismissive of her self-penned stage performance. One reporter wrote, "Too much is still too much, and there is too much Miss West at the Paramount this week. In the picture Mae has all the boys chasing her. On the stage, they're still chasing, one in the flesh, and the others on the telephone. She plays a bad, bad lady who gets more applicants than a want ad."

Mae made her debut on national radio to promote her new film. The only radio appearances she would ever make would be purposed to promote a film or a stage play. On February 2, 1933, she sang an extended version of her signature song, "Frankie and Johnny," on *The Rudy Vallee Hour* (aka *The Fleischmann Yeast Hour*, or *The Fleischmann Hour*), a musical/variety program broadcast on NBC. She was backed up by a male quartette, and the Rudy Vallee orchestra. Fred Astaire and Claude Rains were also guests on the show.

Rudy Vallee introduced her to his massive radio audience. "The newest of movie stars, Miss Mae West. No doubt you saw Miss West in *Night After Night*. Very soon you'll see a great deal more of her in *She Done Him Wrong*, her first starring vehicle on the screen. Whatever Miss West may do in Hollywood, New Yorkers will always remember her for her many sensational plays, particularly for her portrayal of a glamorous heroine in a drama she wrote, directed, and produced herself, *Diamond Lil*. And in *Diamond Lil* one salty episode stands out – Miss West's version of that grand old American folk song, "Frankie and Johnny." Our arranger, Elliot Jacoby, has prepared a dramatic musical setting for this Gay Nineties torch ballad. Put your steriopotican slides back on the what not. Straighten the anamacasm on the old Morris chair. Turn the gas jet low. Lean back and listen to the lamentable history of Frankie and Johnny as related with appropriate gestures by Mae West and company!"

Mae rehearses with the Rudy Vallee Orchestra.

Like many film stars at that time, Mae was approached by a sponsor to do her own weekly radio program in 1934. The actress demanded $7,500 per broadcast. After negotiations, the sponsor agreed to pay her $6,600 per week. As stories about her fierce battles with film censors became the talk of Hollywood, the sponsor, anticipating the dangers of providing Mae West with a live, weekly platform to entertain her public, got cold feet, and canceled the deal. Mae seemed unfazed. Her movie career, which not only involved acting, but writing the scripts as well, kept her too busy to be concerned with creating original material on a weekly basis. She would not return to radio until late in 1937.

NBC's musical-comedy program, *The Chase and Sanborn Hour*, starring ventriloquist Edgar Bergen and his wooden dummy, Charlie McCarthy, was one of the most popular radio programs on the air. The one-hour show featuring actor Don Ameche was broadcast live from the newly opened NBC radio studios at Sunset and Vine in Hollywood. Mae West was booked on the show to promote the upcoming release of her latest film, *Every Day's A Holiday*. She wanted to do a few scenes from the movie, but to save money, the producer of the show wanted to resurrect a Garden of Eden skit that had been done several times before. Mae would interpret the role of Eve, Don Ameche would be Adam, and Edgar Bergen would provide the voice of the duplicitous snake.

The first draft of the script was delivered to Mae on Friday evening, December 10, 1937, preceding the Sunday evening broadcast. She rewrote the script to suit herself and sent it back to the studio on early Saturday morning. The producer rejected her revisions, and brought in veteran comedy writer Arch Oboler to rewrite the script less than twenty-four hours before broadcast. Mae would never agree to play a woman who was subjugated by a man. She insisted that the age-old tale have a feminist twist. Oboler tried to please the actress. "Instead of going on the premise that the snake tempted Eve," he recalled, "it occurred to me, since Miss West was such a dominate woman, to have Eve tempt the snake."

Later that day NBC officials approved Oboler's script. Mae objected, but rehearsed the scenes that evening. The Sunday morning rehearsal was uneventful. The actress seemed a bit cavalier about reading her lines. She purposefully missed the all-important "final dress rehearsal," knowing that the censors might be disturbed by the changes she planned to make for herself, and the way she intended to deliver her lines on the air.

Mae with Charlie McCarthy in her bedroom at her Hollywood apartment.

On December 12, newspapers across the country touted the news that Mae West would make a rare radio appearance on *The Chase and Sanborn Hour* – broadcast live at 8:00 P.M. Eastern Standard Time. Her appearance had been publicized for weeks.

Humorous photographs of Mae reclining in her bed next to Charlie McCarthy had been published in newspapers and magazines leading up to the broadcast.

During the live broadcast, the actress read her lines in her typical, sexy manner which informed the role of Eve in a bawdy way that no one had seen on the written page. Mae's Eve was a discontented wife bored with her complacent husband. She enlists the aid of a treacherous snake to pick a forbidden apple so that she and Adam will be banished from the Garden of Eden. At times it was difficult to hear Mae over the screams and laughter of the live studio audience. Satirizing the beloved Biblical tale of Adam and Eve – and on a Sunday night – caused a firestorm of protest. Before the skit was finished, NBC switchboards across the nation were jammed with calls. As Eve, Mae proclaimed, "If trouble means something that makes your blood run through your veins like seltzer water – Adam, my man, give me trouble!" And it was trouble she got.

The next sketch she performed with Bergen's wooden dummy, Charlie McCarthy, sounded even more shocking than her retelling the story of the Garden of Eden! The producer should have been more concerned with what she intended to do with Charlie. The nation was aghast when she invited him to come home and play in her woodpile! The sketch was actually cut off the air briefly. Listeners' objections were just the beginning. Religious leaders, journalists, civic organizations, women's groups, Parent Teacher Associations and politicians condemned NBC, Chase and Sanborn, the writers, the actors, and Mae West in particular. The movie censors' biggest challenge in Hollywood – Mae West – had rattled radio to its core. She was described as "vulgar," "sacrilegious," "profane," "filthy," "obscene," "blasphemous," and "vomitous." Joseph Breen and the

Legion of Decency – arbiters of movie morals – called for a production code for radio.

Donald O'Toole, a New York Congressman, referred to Mae West as "a certain so-called actress who has served, in the past, a jail sentence for giving an indecent theatrical performance." He stated on the floor of the House of Representatives that the Garden of Eden sketch was an "all time low in this particular field." The Federal Communications Commission considered suspending the licenses of stations that had broadcast the Sunday show. FCC chairman, Frank McNinch, described the Adam and Eve sketch as "offensive to the great mass of right-thinking, clean-minded American citizens." He demanded a copy of the script, which he called "a serious offense against the proprieties, and a rather low form of entertainment."

"Mae West had her day in court," the *New York Sun* editorialized, "her day in film, and now her night on the air. On any other day of the week the skit would have justified the severest criticism from the standpoint of good taste, but on Sunday such a broadcast represents the all-time low in radio."

Rev. Dr. Maurice S. Sheehy, a professor of Religion at Catholic University, described the show as, "the most indecent, scurrilous, and religiously irreverent program that it has ever been my misfortune to hear." His indignant statement regarding the broadcast was introduced into the Congressional Record. Mae had "introduced her own sexual philosophy into the Biblical incident of the fall of man," he wrote. The actress was "the very personification of sex in its lowest connotation." He concluded, "To have this lewd and filthy take-off on the Bible's Adam and Eve was a disgrace!"

Not to be outdone, the Catholic publication, *Monitor*, screamed the headline, "Mae West Pollutes Homes!"

Radio Guide reported, "Mae West has taught radio a lesson. She has demonstrated that what is sauce for the movie goose is not necessarily sauce for the radio gander. Hollywood standards are not Radio City standards. The reason is this: A man can say things in a crowd that he would be ashamed to say before a mother and her son at home."

Martin Quigley wrote in the *Motion Picture Herald*, "Evidence indicates they sent for her. [Mae West was approached by NBC radio, rather than the actress seeking an engagement on the network's show.] She was bought, not sold. A clear-eyed examination of the facts will disclose a daughter of a Brooklyn prizefighter…crystallized into a symbolism of attainable sex, garnished with the ostrich plumes of the red plush parlor period… Mae West got the biggest cocktail hour and smoking compartment line of word-of-mouth publicity in the annals of commercialized fame and the more she got talked about, the more photographs of her in variant degrees of deciduousness appeared in the public prints, the less she was acceptable to the family-communal motion picture audience." About the Adam and Eve sketch, Quigley said, "No religious issue was or is involved. Indecency is indecency in anybody's religion, and it is still indecency even if one has no religion!"

Mae West refused to take the blame for material she claimed she had not written. She said, "The Adam and Eve sketch was an amusing, satirical treatment of the ancient Garden of Eden story. There was nothing offensive in the dialogue or it would never have got on the air in the first place. I only gave the lines my characteristic delivery. What else could I do? I wasn't Aimee Semple McPherson. Or Lincoln at Gettysburg, or John Foster Dulles, or even Eleanor Roosevelt. I was Mae West. Sunday on radio doesn't alter one's personality."

Twenty years later, Mae mused about the uproar in her autobiography, writing, "I had caused a situation of national shock not to be matched till we dropped our first atomic bomb."

NBC defended Mae West initially, stating that she had not written the script or ad-libbed any lines. The J. Walter Thompson advertising agency, which was responsible for the content of the show, took full responsibility for the skits. The network contended that the actress's "delivery and inflection" created the controversy. However, with the public breathing down the neck of the advertiser, and with the FCC threatening to regulate national radio because of Mae West, NBC took to the airwaves the following Sunday evening to apologize for their "mistake." "We share with you the regret you express. Our interests are mutual in giving the American public wholesome entertainment, and we will intensify our efforts to that end." NBC, which controlled fifteen stations, and their fifty-nine affiliates nationwide, agreed to ban Mae West and the mention of her name from their airwaves. Mae would not return to national radio until her appearance on *The Chesterfield Supper Club* hosted by Perry Como in January, 1950.

Even her co-star, Don Ameche, threw her under the bus when he was questioned by Dora Albert for *Modern Screen* magazine. "How did you happen to appear on that broadcast?" she asked the actor. "Did the script read all right?"

Ameche said, "I suppose it didn't, but none of us realized it. I just didn't think. It did not occur to me that a burlesque of Adam and Eve would give offense to many people. If it had occurred to me and I had had any choice about the matter, I certainly would not have appeared on that program. [Ameche was contractually bound to his weekly appearances on *The Chase and Sanborn Hour*.] Of course, as a matter of fact, I have no choice about the lines I read. But if I had realized that the script might be offensive, I should certainly have said something to the director about it. Nearly always when an actor does object to a line, the director will try to have it changed. That is the only time anything like that ever happened to me. I hope nothing like it ever happens again."

Dorothy Lamour, who sang on the program, recalled in her 1980 autobiography, "Our special guest was Mae West who was to play Eve to Don Ameche's Adam in a takeoff on the Bible story. Mae always had it in her contract that she would write her own lines and, as usual, she had inserted some bawdy West-isms. The minute the censors read the script, blue pencils appeared like magic! Mae innocently agreed to all the changes. Then she went on the air and read her script exactly as *she* had written it, word for word! The repercussions were incredible. Church groups were outraged and the mail came pouring in. I can't even remember what she said that was so terrible, but I'm sure it was mild by today's standards."

Rather than contrite, Mae was unrepentant. "Did they expect a sermon?" she opined to the *New York Post* months later on April 25, 1938. "Why weren't they in church if they were so religious? Forty million people listened to that broadcast. That's more people than listened to the abdication of King Edward, even." Her interest was in giving the American public what it wanted. Her controversial appearance on *The Chase and Sanborn Hour*, a show in its sixth year on the air, drew a staggering eighty-four percent share of the listening audience.

The negative publicity affected the box office receipts of *Every Day's A Holiday*. It was the first film she made that lost money. Paramount cancelled their production and distribution deal with

Emanuel Cohen's Major Pictures, which had produced the film. And Cohen, who had originally encouraged a doubtful Mae to appear on the radio program, dropped her film contract, essentially ending her motion picture career. No stranger to controversy, Mae seemed unmoved. She had tired of the constant fights with movie censors, and had no intention of dealing with radio censorship. She turned her attention back to the stage, which successfully occupied her time for the next two decades.

Edgar Bergen, Charlie McCarthy, Mae, Emanuel Cohen and his wife backstage at the NBC radio studios at Sunset and Vine in Hollywood.

The controversial episode of *The Chase and Sanborn Hour* began on a festive, upbeat note when Dorothy Lamour sang the theme song from Mae's film, *Every Day's A Holiday*.

The Adam and Eve sketch unfolded in the Garden of Eden where Adam reclines beneath the spreading branches of a fig tree. Adam and Eve play cards with a deck of fig leaves, but Eve is bored.

EVE	Listen, tall, tan and tired, it's time I told you a thing or two. Ever since creation, I've done nothing but play double solitaire. It's disgustin'! It's got me down!
ADAM	We've got a nice place here.
EVE	That's the trouble! It's too nice!
ADAM	Well, I'm not complaining.
EVE	But I want something to happen! A little excitement! A little adventure! A girl's gotta have a little fun once in a while! There's no future under a fig tree!
ADAM	Now, come on woman. Be like me. Why don't you relax and take it easy?
EVE	'Cause I'm a lady of big ideas.
ADAM	What kind of ideas?
EVE	Oh… you've no idea! Listen, Adam, I've gotta get a chance to expand my personality!
ADAM	Well, go on! Expand!
EVE	I will. Out there.
ADAM	Out there!? You mean outside the gates of the Garden of Eden?
EVE	Now you're talkin'!
ADAM	Well, who knows what's out there?
EVE	I'd like to find out.

ADAM	No. We can't go. We still have a lease on this place.
EVE	You mean to tell me a *lease* is the thing that's holding me back from developing my personality?
ADAM	Well, a lease is a lease! Anyway, we've got a nice place here! Temperature perfect – sun always shining – nothing but a heavy dew once in a while…
EVE	What are yuh? The Chamber of Commerce?
ADAM	Oh, go away and let me sleep, will ya?
EVE	Listen, Adam. I tell yuh, yuh gotta get me out of this place! Yuh gotta break the lease!
ADAM	Now, Eve! This is Eden! Everything is peaceful, and quiet, and safe!
EVE	That's the trouble! It's *too* safe! I tell yuh, it's disgustin'!
ADAM	What are you talking about?
EVE	Adam, yuh don't know a thing about women!
ADAM	Ahh…you apparently forget you were originally one of my own ribs!
EVE	A rib once, but now I'm beefin'!
ADAM	Me – I know everything about women.
EVE	That's coverin' a lot of territory. Listen, long, lazy and lukewarm – yuh think I want to stay in this place all my life!?
ADAM	I do. And I tell you you're one of my ribs!

EVE	Yeah. But one of your floatin' ribs! A couple of months of peace and security and a woman's bored all the way down to the bottom of her marriage certificate.
ADAM	Then what do you want? Trouble?
EVE	Trouble? Listen. If trouble means somethin' that makes yuh catch your breath – if trouble means somethin' that makes your blood run through your veins like seltzer water – Adam, my man, give me trouble!
ADAM	Awww! Eve, you don't want trouble.
EVE	Now tell me the low down truth. Ain't there any way yuh can break our lease?
ADAM	Well, yes there is, but I won't tell you.
EVE	No?
ADAM	No. This is paradise. Free life, free heat, free meals… what else could a man want? Answer me that!
EVE	I got a couple of good ideas if yuh tell me how to break the lease.
ADAM	No. I won't do it.
EVE	Oh, Adam…
ADAM	What?
EVE	Come on over here…

ADAM	What for? To hold hands?
EVE	Oh, that old game? Can't yuh think of somethin' new? Hmmm… yuh know nothin' about nothin'!
ADAM	Oh, yes I do! I know more than you do, woman!
EVE	What, for instance?
ADAM	I know all about the tree.
EVE	What tree, man? What tree?
ADAM	That apple tree in the middle of the garden! The lease says that if we eat any of its fruit, we get thrown out of here!
EVE	Now, is that a fact?
ADAM	Sure! That's why there's a fence around it! I tell you, one bite of those apples and we get a dispossess!
EVE	How fascinatin'! Adam… yuh can hold my hand now…
ADAM	No, I've got a better idea! Come close to me.
EVE	Hmmm… I'm listenin'. I'm waitin'. Well, what're yuh gonna do now?
ADAM	I think I'll go fishing.
EVE	How disgustin'!
ADAM	Now wait a minute! You can't talk to me that way! Why, do you realize I'm man number one!

EVE	Ya, but are yuh number one man?
ADAM	Well…I'll see you around supper time. I'll be back.
EVE	So, that's the trouble… so, it's that tree over there, eh? Hmmm… hello, tree! How would yuh like to do a little lease breakin' for a woman with ideas? Hmmm… not room enough to squeeze through the slats for a woman of my personality. Now if I only knew someone skinny enough…
SNAKE	(hissing) Sssalutationsss, Misssusss Eve!
EVE	Oh…Well, hello Mr. Snake! Hello, long, dark, and slinky…
SNAKE	Misssusss Eve, why are you ssstanding by that tree?
EVE	Stop wigglin' and I'll tell yuh. Listen, I know yuh don't approve of me, but I've got a little proposition to make!
SNAKE	I sssertainly refussse to lisssten! (pause) What isss it?
EVE	Do you think with the proper provocation yuh could squeeze through that fence there around that tree?
SNAKE	That'sss the forbidden tree!
EVE	Don't be technical! Answer me this – could yuh get those snake hips of yours through those pickets?
SNAKE	I won't go through a picket line!

EVE	Now look here, my palpitatin' python – would yuh like to have this whole paradise to yourself?
SNAKE	Ssssertainly!
EVE	Okay, then pick me a handful of fruit. Adam and I'll eat it. And the Garden of Eden is all yours! Now, what do yuh say?
SNAKE	Ssssoundsss alright… but it'sss forbidden fruit!
EVE	Listen. What are yuh? My friend in the grass, or a snake in the grass?
SNAKE	But forbidden fruit!
EVE	Are yuh a snake or are yuh a mouse?
SNAKE	I'll do it… I'll do it.
EVE	Now you're talkin'! Here… right in between these pickets!
SNAKE	I'm… I'm ssstuck!
EVE	Shake your hips! There! You're through!
SNAKE	Oh… I ssshouldn't be doing thisss!
EVE	But you're doin' alright! Get me a big one! I feel like doin' a Big Apple!
SNAKE	Here you are, Misssusss Eve.
EVE	Hmmm… I see… Nice goin' swivel hips!
SNAKE	Wait a minute! It won't work! Adam will never eat that forbidden apple!

EVE	Oh, yes he will. When I'm through with it!
SNAKE	Nonsssense. He won't!
EVE	He will if I feed him like women'll feed men for the rest of time!
SNAKE	What'sss that?
EVE	Applesauce!

MUSICAL BRIDGE

ADAM	Eve! Where are you, Eve?
EVE	Hmmm... waitin' my love, jus' waitin'!
ADAM	Hello, Eve. What have you been doing?
EVE	Me? I've just been makin' a little bit of history!
ADAM	Huh?
EVE	The first woman to make a monkey out of snake!
ADAM	Say, how about supper? Don't tell me we've got fig stew again!?
EVE	No. Somethin' new, so help me, somethin' new! Here! Have a bite of this.
ADAM	What? What is it?
EVE	A new kind of sauce. Good for yuh.
ADAM	Are you sure?
EVE	Just to prove it's pure and unadulterated one hundred percent proof, I'll have a demitasse of it m'self! All right... no, wait... before you eat... an-

	swer me this. Are yuh going to take me out of this dismal dump and give me a chance to develop… my personality?
ADAM	Aw, Eve… are you going to start that over again?
EVE	No. I'm goin' to end it! Eat your sauce, big boy, and hold your hat – if you've got one!
ADAM	Say… this is darn good sauce! Where did you…
	SUDDEN CRASH OF THUNDER – BLOWING WIND – MUSIC PAINTING A PICTURE OF PANDEMONIUM – RISING AND FALLING – WHISTLE ENDING WITH A DULL BOOM
ADAM	My… my head… where… what… what happened to me?
EVE	We've been dispossessed!
ADAM	But… but why?
EVE	Forbidden applesauce!
ADAM	Oh, Eve… what have you done?
EVE	I've just made a little more history, that's all. I'm the first woman to have her own way – and a snake'll take the rap for it!
ADAM	But, Eve… we've lost the Garden of Eden! We're…
	MUSIC BEGINS BUILDING BEHIND
ADAM	(Cont.) Eve! It's…it's as if I see you for the first time! You're beautiful!

EVE	Hmmm... yuh fascinate me!
ADAM	Your eyes!
EVE	Tell me more!
ADAM	Your... your lips! Come closer... I wanna hold you close! I wanna...
EVE	Yuh wanna what?
	SOUND OF A GREAT, LONG KISS – FOLLOWED BY A GREAT CRASH.
ADAM	Eve! What was that!?
EVE	That was ...the original kiss!
	MUSIC. THE END

NBC switchboards were ablaze with calls from shocked listeners, but the broadcast could not be stopped. It was too late. In the next skit with Ameche, Bergen and McCarthy, Mae was about to curl the hair of all the listeners!

DON	Ladies and gentlemen! At last the long awaited meeting of siren Mae West and Casanova Charles McCarthy has arrived. This is a romantic battle of the century – the dramatic moment that millions have been looking forward to! Tension is riding high, and so are the bets! The odds are Mae West five, Charlie McCarthy three! There is some talk that Charlie will weaken! They say no man can resist her! But there are others who feel that Charlie will vanquish the vampire! Wait a minute! Wait a

minute! Last minute flash! There's been a drop in the odds! Mae West four, Charlie McCarthy four and a half! Let's get a word from the challenger, Charlie McCarthy.

Bergen, McCarthy, and Mae.

DON	What have you got to say, Charlie?
CHARLIE	It looks like a tough fight, Don, but I'll win.
DON	Why do you say it's a tough fight?
CHARLIE	Well, my opponent's in great form. She's had lots of training.
DON	What do you think your chances are to win?
CHARLIE	Well, I've had some great fights in the east.
DON	What do you think of the West?

CHARLIE	Mighty pretty country. Mighty pretty.
DON	Well, Charlie's never been in better condition. He's a fashion plate with his midnight blue full dress suit, top hat and monocle, and a blue white butterfly tie and dress shirt.
CHARLIE	It's P. K.
DON	P.K. tie and shirt.
CHARLIE	Ya, shot with gravy.
DON	And now a word from the champion, Mae West. We've heard so much about you, Miss West. Won't you say a word?
MAE	Well, all I got to say is, where there's smoke, there's fire.
CHARLIE	Wow! Boy she burns me up!
MAE	There's nothin' I like better than the aroma of burnin' wood.
CHARLIE	I wonder if she means me?
DON	Better watch out Charlie. Say, Charlie, do you smell that perfume?
CHARLIE	Yes.
DON	Isn't it ravishing?
CHARLIE	Yes, it is! It's ravishing! It's weakening! So help me, I'm swooning! What is it?

Mae and Charlie.

MAE Why, it's my favorite perfume. *Ashes of Men*.

CHARLIE Oh…oh. *Ashes of Men*? Holy smoke. She's not going to make a cinder out of me.

BERGEN Well, Don, there's been a great deal of talk, but very little action so far.

DON Right you are, Edgar! Miss West, this is the famous Charlie McCarthy.

MAE Hello, short, dark, and handsome.

CHARLIE Hello, tall, blond, and terrific!

BERGEN Charlie! That's no way to talk to Miss West. You hardly know her.

CHARLIE I know it Bergen. I'm a cad. I hate myself.

Mae and Charlie, with Edgar Bergen.

MAE   Oh, listen, Charlie, are these your keys?

CHARLIE   Oh, thanks Mae, did I leave them in the car?

MAE   No. Yuh left them in my apartment!

CHARLIE   Oh… oh. Looks like we're going to have a white Christmas… (sings) Oh, jingle bells, jingle bells…

BERGEN   Charlie, where did you leave those keys?

CHARLIE   I… oh… ah…

BERGEN   Where did you leave those keys?

CHARLIE   I… oh… ah…

MAE   He left them on my dresser. So what? Charlie, why don't yuh walk out on Bergen? What's holdin' yuh?

CHARLIE   Well, he is. You'd better tell him Mae.

Mae and Charlie with Edgar Bergen in Mae's bedroom.

MAE   All right, if yuh wanna know, he did come up to see me.

BERGEN   Oh, he did!? And what was he doing up there?

MAE   Well, Charlie came up, an' I showed him my etchings. An' he showed me his stamp collection.

CHARLIE   There you have it, Bergen, there you have it.

BERGEN   Yes. So that's all there was to it… etchings and a stamp collection?

CHARLIE   Ha, ha… he's so naïve!

MAE   So, that's what's the matter with him? Come here honey. Closer, so we can talk intimately.

CHARLIE	If you don't mind, I think I better keep my distance.
MAE	Well, I don't like long distance conversations, so come here. I thought we were gonna have a nice long talk Tuesday night at my apartment. Where did yuh go when the doorbell rang?
CHARLIE	Well, I tried to hide in your clothes closet, but two guys kicked me out. So, I went out the back door.
MAE	Don't tell me yuh went down… uh, out the French windows!? I'm on the third floor, y' know!
CHARLIE	Oh, so that's what it was, the French windows, huh? I was gonna say you were pretty skimpy with those back steps!
MAE	Yuh look pretty good to me, Charlie. Come here.
CHARLIE	But I thought you only liked tall men.
MAE	Oh, that was my last year's model. This year I'm on a diet.
CHARLIE	Oh, so that's it. She's on a diet.
BERGEN	Yes. Tell me Miss West, have you ever found the one man in your life that you could really love?
MAE	Sure. Lots 'a times!
CHARLIE	Could you even like Mr. Bergen?
MAE	Ah… Mr. Bergen. Of course. He's very sweet. In fact, he's a right guy. Confidentially, yuh'll have to show me a man I don't like.

Mae and Charlie in Mae's bed.

CHARLIE	That's swell! Bergen's your man! You know, he can be had!
MAE	On second thought, I'm liable to take him away from yuh. Then what'll yuh say?
CHARLIE	Well, if you take Bergen away, I'm speechless.
MAE	Yuh meant to say I'd do yuh wrong?
CHARLIE	Well, now that you ask…
MAE	Or are yuh afraid I'd do yuh right?
CHARLIE	Well, I'm kind of confused. I need time for that one, Mae.
MAE	That's alright. I like a man what takes his time. Why don't yuh come up… uh, home with me now, honey? I'll let yuh play in my woodpile.
CHARLIE	Well, I'm not feeling so well tonight. I've been feeling nervous lately. I think I'm gonna have a

nervous breakdown. Whuup! There I go!

MAE So, good-time Charlie's gonna play hard to get! Well, yuh can't kid me. You're afraid of women. Your Casanova stuff is just a front! A false front!

CHARLIE Not so loud, Mae! Not so loud! All my girlfriends are listening!

MAE Oh, yeah? You're all wood and a yard long…

CHARLIE Yeah.

MAE Yuh weren't so nervous and backward when yuh came up to see me at my apartment. In fact, yuh didn't need any encouragement to kiss me!

CHARLIE Did I do that?

Mae and Charlie in her Ravenswood bedroom.

MAE Why, yuh certainly did! I got marks to prove it! An' splinters, too!

CHARLIE   Oh, that's too much! This is too much!

MAE   Well, get this! I don't need yuh! I got all the gentleman friends I want! I got men for every mood! Men for every day of the week… Monday, Tuesday, Wednesday, Thursday, and good man Friday, and a good man Saturday! I change my men like I change my clothes. And you… and you…

CHARLIE   Mae! Mae! You're not walking out on me are you?

MAE   I've got a reputation at stake! No man walks out on me, they might carry them out, but they never walk out!

CHARLIE   I'm mad about you! I love you! I've acted like a fool!

MAE   That wasn't acting. Come here. I'll show yuh how to act!

CHARLIE   Mae! Mae! Don't be so rough… To me love is peace and quiet!

MAE   That ain't love, that's sleep!

CHARLIE   Oh… oh… Mae! Mae! Cut it out… Mae… Mae… help! Bergen help!

MAE   Oh, call Bergen! Call everybody! I don't need any help!

MUSIC

THE END

Charlie McCarthy and Mae West.

CHAPTER 2

Mail Call Almost

"I'm glad to be here for the boys."

IN 1944, *RADIO DAILY* published a story written by Lt. Col. Thomas A.H. Lewis, the commander of the Armed Forces Radio Service. "The initial production of the Armed Forces Radio Service was *Mail Call*," wrote Lewis, "a morale-building half hour which brought famed performers to the microphone to sing and gag in the best American manner. To a fellow who has spent months guarding an outpost in the South Seas, Iceland or Africa a cheery greeting from a favorite comedian, a song hit direct from Broadway, or the beating rhythm of a hot band, mean a tie with the home to which he hopes soon to return."

Mail Call was first broadcast in August, 1942 from the organization's headquarters at 6011 Santa Monica Boulevard in Hollywood. Lt. Col. Lewis had been vice-president of a prestigious Hollywood advertising agency and had access to top Hollywood talent. The program featured the biggest film, stage, and music stars of the day, and was recorded and internationally broadcast specifically for the various branches of the American, and Allied Armed Forces. Some of the programs were syndicated for CBS radio.

On October 21, 1944, *The Billboard* magazine reported that, "The four top armed forces radio service shows, *Command Performance*, *Mail Call*, *Jubilee*, and *G.I. Journal* will be cut in New York from October 15 until November 13, a total of more than 12 shows. Idea is to give G.I.'s a chance to hear Eastern legit and night club talent."

In November, 1944, Mae West was starring in her Broadway hit, *Catherine Was Great*. Twenty-eight-year old Frank Sinatra was riding the wave of singing stardom. His October engagement at the Paramount Theater in Manhattan caused his bobby-soxer fans to riot in the streets.

Considering the prevailing radio ban that prevented Mae from performing on national radio, it's not known if Mae and Frank actually recorded their sketch for *Mail Call* which was scheduled for broadcast on November 9, 1944. Singer Gertrude Niesen hosted the November 9th program with guest Frank Sinatra and the Benny Goodman Quintet, but no recording of the West/Sinatra sketch seems to exist. The script is the only historical record of the most unusual – and missing – pairing of Mae West and Frank Sinatra.

Mail Call

GERTRUDE …Now as we continue our little get together with the stars of the Big Town, we turn left on Forty-Fifth Street West of Broadway to the stage door of the Royale Theatre. The curtain is coming down on the hit show *Catherine Was Great*. The star has just taken her last curtain call and is walking off the stage toward her dressing room. Fellas… it's MAE WEST!

LONG PLAY ON… APPLAUSE

GERTRUDE Welcome to *Mail Call*, Miss West!

MAE I'm glad to be here for the boys.

GERTRUDE I know that millions of men all over the world will be thrilled at hearing your voice!

MAE My voice? Too bad I couldn't contribute a little more… you know, I've spent a lot of time with servicemen…

GERTRUDE Really!?

MAE Yes. And I found that each branch of the service has its own technique. A soldier waits ten minutes before he puts his arm around you…

Mae is officially accepted as a member of the Royal Air Force Mae West Club by two ranking members, RAF fliers Kenneth Baird (left) and Eric Bostock (right), who visited her in Hollywood. The fliers are wearing "Mae West" lifebelts. During WWII, allied soldiers called the type B-4 inflatable life jackets "Mae West" in honor of her buxom figure.

GERTRUDE   Uh, huh…

MAE   A sailor will wait five minutes…

GERTRUDE   What about the Marines?

MAE   They've already landed.

GERTRUDE	Well, that takes care of the Army, the Navy, and the Marines. Now, how about a Coastguardsman?
MAE	No thanks. I just left one.
GERTRUDE	I see. You know, here on *Mail Call* no request is too big or too small. And we just got a request from Carl Oakman at A.P.O. 451.
MAE	What does the boy want?
GERTRUDE	Carl wants you to do one of those famous Mae West love scenes.
MAE	But this is only a half hour show! Hardly gives me time to warm up my motor… besides, what am I going to use for a leading man?
GERTRUDE	We happen to have one right here. Fellas… here's FRANK SINATRA!
	APPLAUSE
GERTRUDE	Miss West, this is Frank Sinatra.
MAE	Hmmm… So you're the Voice, huh?
FRANK	Yes, ma'am.
MAE	Ya? Well, meet the body. So, he's going to be my leading man today?
GERTRUDE	Yes. It looks like the fates have sent you a lover.
MAE	How do you like those fates… they send a boy to do a man's work.

FRANK	Wait a minute, Mae! You're talking to a man… a real he-man.
MAE	A he-man has hair on his chest.
FRANK	Well, I got hair on my chest. Just take a look.
MAE	I don't see a thing.
FRANK	Oh, darn it! I forgot to put the mascara on today! Please, Mae, Please! Try to understand. Ever since the first time I saw you I wanted to grab you in my arms, crush you to me, and squeeze you tighter and tighter and tighter.
MAE	Hmmm… this boy's got possibilities. Tell me, does your vitamin pill taste different lately?
FRANK	Please, Mae. I'm serious. You leave me breathless.
MAE	Honey, that's how I found you. But let's cut down on the small talk. We've had a request to do a little love scene… and hot or cold, ready or not, you're gonna be my man.
FRANK	What a thrill! Hearing that from a girl past fourteen!
MAE	Well, stick around, tall, dark, and meatless… I've chosen as our vehicle a little thing called *Romeo and Juliet*…
FRANK	Oh, Goody! I hope I'm Romeo!
MAE	I hope you are, too… as the scene opens, I'm up on the balcony, and you're down in the garden. A little Shakespearean music, please…

MUSIC UP: "ALL OR NOTHING AT ALL" PLAYS AND SLOWLY FADES OUT

MAE   Romeo, Romeo, wherefore art thou, Romeo?

FRANK   I'm down here in the Victory Garden, Juliet.

MAE   Well, dig up some spinach, you're gonna need your strength tonight.

FRANK   Ah, my Juliet. Wilst thou be mine?

MAE   Wilst.

FRANK   Wouldst thou elope with me?

MAE   Wouldst.

FRANK   Then tell me wherest, whenest, and howest. Juliet, let us elope this very moment.

MAE   I cannot, my Romeo. Daddy has locked me in.

FRANK   Well, jump from the balcony and I'll catch you in my arms.

MAE   This boy is toying with total destruction.

FRANK   Well, if you don't come down, I'll climb up to your balcony on this rose bush…

SOUND: FAST ASCENDING SLIDE WHISTLE AND A LOUD THUD.

MAE   How'd you get up here so fast?

FRANK   I backed into a thorn.

MAE   Well, now that you're up here, there must be something we can do.

FRANK	May I hold your hand?
MAE	Listen, slugger… never mind the preliminaries, let's get to the main bout.
FRANK	You mean you want me to kiss you?
MAE	Certainly.
FRANK	But I never kissed a girl before. In the game of love, my lips are rookies.
MAE	Well, I'd like 'em to meet a couple that have been through basic training, so how about that kiss, Romeo?
FRANK	Okay. I'll take you in my arms and bend you back and kiss you! I'll bend you back further… and further…
MAE	Please… let's not tilt the machine!
FRANK	I'm sorry, Juliet. When I'm with you, I get all jittery. I feel like a kid in kindergarten.
MAE	Kindergarten, eh? Here, let me show you how it's done…
	SOUND OF MAE AND FRANK PASSIONATELY KISSING.
FRANK	Wow! I just got my PHD! Ah, my Juliet. To prove my love, let me sing to you… a song called, "I Love You."
MAE	Sing, Romeo… but I better get off this balcony. I may swoon and fall right on my bobby sock.

MUSIC: FRANK SINGS "I LOVE YOU."

APPLAUSE

GERTRUDE Thank you, Mae West and Frank Sinatra! I'm sure that every G.I. everywhere got a big kick out of that!

THE END

Mae West in 1944.

The Chesterfield Supper Club.

CHAPTER 3

The Chesterfield Supper Club

"Just like baseball, a man is safe at home."

IN THE FEBRUARY 1937 issue of *Movie Classic* magazine, Mae West was asked (a bit prematurely), "What do you think of television?" She answered, "I'd like it – it would give me a chance to come up and see you sometime."

Not surprisingly, the actress was ahead of her time. Experimental television broadcasting began in France in the 1930s. In the United States, four television networks (NBC, CBS, ABC, and DuMont), broadcasting over 128 stations, began a full-time, seven-days-a-week, prime time schedule in 1948. In the early days of television, performances, teleplays, and programs were broadcast live. The FCC, which controlled the content – what could and could not be broadcast on the radio, and later, television – had banned Mae West from the airwaves after her radio appearance with Charlie McCarthy. She wouldn't be considered for television for the next fifteen years.

Mae West's ban from national radio ended in January, 1950, when NBC offered her an olive branch with trepidation. She was starring in a successful and critically acclaimed production of her play, *Diamond Lil*, at the Plymouth Theater in New York when she agreed to appear on the long-running hit radio program, *The Chesterfield Supper Club*. John Mason Brown wrote in the *Saturday Review*, "Only the Statue of Liberty has been carrying a torch for a longer time than Mae West. She, moreover, seems no more fatigued by maintaining her chosen attitude than does the iron lady down the bay with her eternally uplifted hand."

The actress was experiencing renewed interest in her life and career. In 1949, Sheridan House publishing company reissued her two novels, *Diamond Lil* and *The Constant Sinner*. And Decca Records released a boxed set of her songs. Paramount tried to re-release her two most popular films *She Done Him Wrong* and *I'm No Angel*, but Joseph Breen, enforcer of Hollywood's Production Code, denied the request. It was baffling, but Breen still insisted Mae West was too hot for movie audiences to handle in 1950. "No good will accrue to the industry among the right-thinking people with a release of a Mae West picture."

Mae's appearance with Perry Como would provide her with a platform to advertise *Diamond Lil*, which was scheduled to begin a national tour in several weeks. Singer Perry Como hosted and starred in the radio show. Popular disc jockey Martin Block was the program's on-air announcer. Mitchell Ayres directed the orchestra, and the Fontane Sisters serenaded the listeners.

Recorded at NBC's Studio 8H at Radio City, the program was recorded on Tuesday, January 3, and broadcast two days later on Thursday evening, January 5, 1950. The two-day delay gave the censors the opportunity to "blue bleach" any questionable material.

On January 16, *Newsweek* reported that the small studio audience was treated to the visual spectacle of the actress, who was "garbed in a bandage-white beaded evening gown cut to reveal a discreet midriff, with reflections from an enormous diamond lavaliere and ring lighting her way."

Perry Como with Mae West on the air.

The January 5th broadcast began:

> MUSIC SWELLS, ORCHESTRA PLAYS "FRANKIE AND JOHNNY" AS MAE WEST ENTERS.

PERRY   It's good to see you, Miss West.

MAE   You're not bad to look at yourself.

PERRY   Thank you. You really look wonderful in that beautiful dress, and those diamonds…

MAE   The dress warms them up and the ice cools them off.

PERRY	You know that could give a guy pneumonia, but what a wonderful way to go…
MAE	Say, there's something that's got a pungent odor around here.
PERRY	Oh, that's me! It's a new cologne I'm wearing called, *My Crime*.
MAE	It certainly is.
PERRY	I'm sorry if you don't like it.
MAE	Why don't you try some of mine?
PERRY	What's it called?
MAE	*Panther Passion.*
PERRY	*Panther Passion?*
MAE	One whiff and you leap!
PERRY	I'm afraid that's too powerful for me!
MAE	All you need is a little drop behind each ear.
PERRY	Okay, I'll try some.
MAE	There. How's that?
PERRY	Hey, that's not bad at all. (whistles)
MAE	Just like the bottle says… guaranteed to bring a wolf to the door!
PERRY	But I'm no wolf. I'm a perfect gentleman.
MAE	Which are you? Perfect or a gentleman?

PERRY   Well, I…

MITCHELL   Say, Perry. How about introducing me?

PERRY   Oh, sure. Miss West, I'd like you to meet Mitchell Ayres.

MITCHELL   Hello, Miss West.

MAE   Hmmm… Mr. Ayres.

PERRY   He's a big one, isn't he?

MAE   Hmmm… ya. Too bad I'm on a diet right now.

MITCHELL   Say, Perry. I think I better get back to the orchestra. It's getting kind of warm over here.

PERRY   Okay, Mitch.

MAE   He's the kind you gotta keep in a home freezer.

MARTIN   Hey, Perry? How about me?

PERRY   Oh, of course. Miss West this is Martin Block.

MAE   Hmmm… Mr. Block.

MARTIN   Hello, Miss West. What do you say? How about a date sometime?

MAE   Date? I'll have to put you on my waiting list.

PERRY   Look. You'll have to excuse Mitch and Martin. But men will be men.

MAE   I wouldn't want them to be anything else!

PERRY   Let's talk about you, Mae. This is a real event having you here on radio.

MAE	And I'm glad it was you that asked me, Perry. You know your voice has always fascinated me.
PERRY	It's nice to hear you say that.
MAE	I buy all your records, but I can't keep them very long.
PERRY	Why not?
MAE	After I listen to you sing, and I take the record off the phonograph, the wax melts.
PERRY	Maybe you have too much steam in your apartment.
MAE	Steam?! In my apartment?!
PERRY	I see what you mean, Mae. And I'm also a great fan of yours. I saw you in your hit show *Diamond Lil*. You were wonderful!
MAE	Thank you.
PERRY	You know, Mae, you not only did some fine acting in *Diamond Lil*, you did some pretty terrific sinning… I mean singing!
MAE	Hmmm… I see what you mean…
PERRY	So how about doing a song for us?
MAE	Well, I'd rather hear you sing. I told you your voice fascinated me.
PERRY	Well…
MAE	And when I get fascinated… anything might happen…

PERRY	Okay. The Fontane Sisters and I will do our version of "I Wanna Go Home With You."
MAE	Swell!
PERRY	Wait a minute. Wait a minute… I forgot the three girls aren't here. So it looks like you'll have to take their place. Would you mind, Mae?
MAE	Not at all. I've taken the place of three women before!
PERRY	Okay, Mitchell, give us a down beat.
	MUSIC BEGINS. "I WANNA GO HOME (WITH YOU)"
PERRY	Mae, you wouldn't want to take a ride in the car, would you?
MAE	No.
PERRY	You wouldn't want to go down to the corner and have an ice cream cone, would you?
MAE	No. Say, what are you leading up to, honey?
PERRY	(singing) "I wanna go home with you…"
MAE	It's a little early isn't it?
PERRY	(singing) "I wanna go home with you…"
MAE	Just like baseball. A man is safe at home.
PERRY	(singing) "I want to meet the family…"
MAE	But I live alone.

PERRY	(singing) "Nobody else will do."
MAE	Do what?
PERRY	(singing) "Kiss me goodnight at your front door, makes me love you more and more…"
MAE	Did you ever try kissing in a revolving door?
PERRY	(singing) "I want to go with you."
MAE	A man in the house is worth two on the street any time!
PERRY	(singing) "I want to go with you…"
	FADE OUT. END SCENE.
PERRY	Mae, you know that was a lot of fun.
MAE	Perry, you being in that category makes me want to do things to you…
PERRY	Now's your chance, because right here is where you and I are going to do *Romeo and Juliet*.
MAE	Hmmm…
PERRY	All right, Martin, will you set the scene?
	TRUMPETS BLARE
MARTIN	*The Chesterfield Supper Club* presents *Romeo and Juliet*. Starring Mae West and Perry Como. Produced by Mae West. Directed by Mae West. And Approved by Mae West. From an idea by William Shakespeare.

MUSIC OVERTURE

PERRY   What light through yonder window breaks? It is the sun, and Juliet is the sun.

MAE   Oh, Comeo. Where for art thou, Comeo?

PERRY   Down here in yonder orchard below your balcony.

MAE   Why don't you come up and see me sometime?

PERRY   But Juliet, the orchard walls are high and hard to climb.

MAE   Alright, forget the balcony. We'll meet on the mezzanine.

PERRY   Ah, yes, but can we smoke on the mezzanine?

MAE   At a time like this you think of Chesterfields!?

PERRY   Juliet, fair Juliet, let me hear thine voice once more.

MAE   Okay.

PERRY   She speaks! Oh, speak again bright angel!

MAE   I may be bright, but I ain't no angel!

PERRY   Juliet, I love thee!

MAE   Not an original statement, but I like it!

PERRY   Dear Juliet…

MAE   Quiet Comeo. I hear some noise from within my room.

PERRY   Maybe it is a mouse within your room.

MAE	I shall go and see.
PERRY	Do not fear, Juliet, whether it be man or mouse.
MAE	If it's a mouse, I'll call for help.
PERRY	Oh, blessed, blessed night. I'm afeard being in night. All this is but a dream… but what a dream…
MAE	Hey, Comeo.
PERRY	Yes, my dear.
MAE	It's almost dawn. I better not have thee hanging around my balcony.
PERRY	I wilst depart immediately. My mule train awaits.
MAE	Parting is such sweet sorrow, but if I know my man, he'll be back tomorrow…
PERRY	And now I goest, fair Juliet.
MAE	Oh don't go. Baby, it's cold outside. Why not come in and have some hot chocolate… very hot.
PERRY	Yeh! And merrily… wait a minute, Mae. Shakespeare kept the two lovers apart!
MAE	Would you rather do it his way, or mine? Come in…
	SEGUE
PERRY	Mae that was really wonderful, and before you go, I'd like you to give us a little advice.
MAE	Advice? Advice about what?

PERRY	Well, about selling Chesterfields.
MAE	Oh, if it's about Chesterfields, okay. Well, I'd say Chesterfields are… hmmm… hmmm… hmmm…
PERRY	What do you mean Chesterfields are hmmm… hmmm… hmmm…
MAE	Hmmm much milder… hmmm much better tasting… hmmm much fuller smoking…
PERRY	Hmmm… you're so right.
MAE	Why, every man I know smokes Chesterfields, and that's a lot of men!
PERRY	What about the women? Women smoke Chesterfields, too!
MAE	The women? Well, that's your department. So long, and thanks a million!
PERRY	So long Mae and thank you very much for being with us!

THE END

Not surprisingly, Mae's appearance on *The Chesterfield Supper Club* drew high ratings for the program. Times had changed, but Mae West had not. Fans loved hearing her again on the radio, and critics raved about her brash, unbounded humor. Weeks later, as *Diamond Lil* was about to embark on tour, Mae appeared again with Perry Como. The program was broadcast on February 16, 1950.

Mae West with actor James Courtney on stage in *Diamond Lil,* 1950.

ANNOUNCER   There is a difference between Chesterfield and other cigarettes. Mae West knows the difference. Do you?

    MUSIC OVERTURE

ANNOUNCER   *Chesterfield Supper Club* starring Perry Como, and his special guest, Mae West!

    MUSIC. FONTANE SISTERS sing lead-in.

PERRY   Tonight, we're expecting Mae West.

MITCH   Yahoo!!

PERRY   Quiet, Mitchell. Ever since she was here last January I've been trying to get her to come back and see us again.

BEA FONTANE   How are you making out?

PERRY   Well, Bea, I sent her a big box of candy and two dozen American Beauty Roses.

BEA   What happened?

PERRY   She sent them back with this note; Dear Perry, I never allow a man to give me candy or flowers. P.S. why not try diamonds?

BEA   And did you?

PERRY   Did I? I went over to Harry Altman's and I picked out the biggest diamond I could find. It was so big it took three strong men to carry it over to her house.

MITCH   But, Perry. She is coming, isn't she?

PERRY   Supper clubbers! The fabulous Mae West!

MUSIC LEAD-IN "FRANKIE AND JOHNNY." MAE WEST enters.

PERRY   Ah, Miss West. You're as beautiful as ever. Pretty as a picture.

MAE   What are you lookin' at? The picture or the frame?

PERRY	Those diamonds! Brother, what beautiful diamonds!
MAE	Brother had nothin' to do with it, honey!
PERRY	I never saw such diamonds! You must have robbed a bank!
MAE	No, but the banker's son is always nice to me.
PERRY	Mae, since this isn't television, I wonder if you could tell our listeners something about your diamonds. For instance, what's the big one around your neck?
MAE	Well, that's the Maximilian diamond. It's 35 carats. My earrings are 28 carats each. And this here ring is 24 carats. And this little… oh… how'd that get in here. (She removes the ring and tosses it away to the loud SOUND of shattering glass.)
PERRY	Well, Mae, I'm awfully glad you're here. I had quite a time finding you. I guess you're out on the road with your show, *Diamond Lil*.
MAE	Ya, we're taking a little tour up to Rochester, Cleveland, and on up to Toronto.
PERRY	Toronto, Canada? It's pretty cold up there.
MAE	Ya, but they won't notice the cold as soon as I get there.
PERRY	When you appeared on the *Supper Club* last

	January, you caused so much excitement that I just had to find you.
MAE	Oh. That's what they all say…
PERRY	No, this I mean. Didn't you see all the stories in the papers and magazines?
MAE	Yes, I did. And I would personally like to thank all the gentlemen of the press for the wonderful things they said about me.
PERRY	Why don't you thank them?
MAE	Thanks, boys!
PERRY	Well, you certainly did things to Mitch Ayres when you were on the show!
MAE	I did?
PERRY	When you said that Chesterfields are… hmmm… hmmm… hmmm…
MAE	Yes?
PERRY	He hasn't been the same since!
MAE	Couldn't take it?
PERRY	That's why I wanted you to… come up and see me.
MAE	I like the way you say that.
PERRY	Mae, look. I really need your help.
MAE	What can I do for you, Perry?

PERRY	Since you said that, Mitch hasn't slept a wink!
MAE	Why doesn't he try sleeping on the edge of his bed?
PERRY	Edge of the bed?
MAE	That way he might drop off!
PERRY	Mae, this is a very serious thing. The poor guy is going crazy. He's getting bags under his eyes. He's nervous, exhausted… but he just can't stop thinking about you. Something's got to be done!
MAE	Hmmm… maybe I could tell him a bedtime story.
PERRY	Do you tell bedtime stories?!
MAE	Ya…
PERRY	That will do it! It will either put him to sleep permanently, or keep him walking the floor for the rest of his life.
MAE	Perry, I'll need your help in telling this story.
PERRY	My help?!
MAE	Ya, I think I'll tell him the story of *Little Red Riding Hood*, and you can play the part of the Wolf.
PERRY	Yes. Now, Mae, while Martin is getting the cast ready, maybe we can sing a duet?
MAE	I'd rather hear you sing, and I'll just listen.
PERRY	All right, Billy Boy, would you play something on the piano, nice and pretty?

MUSIC BEGINS. "I'M IN THE MOOD FOR LOVE."

PERRY: (singing) "I'm in the mood for love…"

MAE: Who isn't?

PERRY: (singing) "Simply because you're near me…"

MAE: That's reason enough!

PERRY: (singing) "Funny, but when you're near me, I'm in the mood for love…"

MAE: You've got a one track mind, but you're on the right track!

PERRY: (singing) "Why stop to think of whether, this little dream might fade…"

MAE: Why stop for anything?

PERRY: (singing) "We'll put our hearts together, and they are one, I'm not afraid…"

MAE: Afraid of what?

PERRY: (singing) "Though there are clouds above…"

MAE: What are you looking up there for?!

PERRY: (singing) "If it should rain, we'll let it…"

MAE: Oh, let it pour!

PERRY: (singing) "But for tonight, forget it, 'cause I'm in the mood…"

MAE: Mood for what?

PERRY	(singing) "I'm in the mood…"
MAE	Honey, you just said that!
	MUSIC FADES
PERRY	Mae, can't we just play some canasta?
MAE	Alright, Perry, start dealing!
	SEGUE
PERRY	Now I think it's about time to put Mitch Ayres to sleep, so if Mae West is ready, I'm ready. Martin, will you set the scene for Mae West's bedtime story entitled, *Little Red Riding Hood*.
	ORCHESTRA PLAYS "ROCK A BYE BABY."
MARTIN	Once upon a time, there lived a little girl named Little Red Riding Hood. One day her mother said to her, child your grandma is very sick. Now you take this basket of food to her house in the forest. So Little Red Riding Hood set forth through the woods with the basket on her arm. It was a bright, sunny day, and as Little Red Riding Hood skipped along, she began to sing a nursery song.
MAE	(singing) "Frankie and Johnny were lovers…"
MARTIN	Then, all of a sudden, a great big wolf caught sight of her. And the wolf took one look at Little Red Riding Hood, and he said to himself.
PERRY	(cat whistles)
MARTIN	All at once, the wolf jumped out of his hiding

	place right in front of the little girl. When Little Red Riding Hood saw this great big wolf, of course she was very, very frightened, so she said…
MAE	Hi ya, tall, tan, and tantalizing.
MARTIN	And the wolf said…
PERRY	Hello there, little girl, and who might you be?
MAE	The name's Little Red Riding Hood. Who are you?
PERRY	Don't you recognize me? I'm the wolf!
MAE	Well, I didn't think you were Rudolph the Red Nosed Reindeer!
PERRY	Where are you bound for, honey?
MAE	I'm on my way to my sick old grandma. But I could be talked out of it!
PERRY	Well…
MAE	You convinced me!
PERRY	Oh, no, no! If your grandma's sick, I'm going to hurry over to see her. Goodbye, Little Red Riding Hood.
MAE	Hmmm… he passes me up to see my grandma! He ain't no wolf, he's a dove!
	MUSICAL SEGUE
MARTIN	Ah, but the wolf was very foxy. He ran quickly to grandma's house and ate up the poor old lady all in one gulp! Then, he put on the old grandma's night

	cap and climbed into bed to wait for Little Red Riding Hood, and very soon he heard her coming up the path.
MAE	(singing, knocks on grandma's door) "How come you do me like you do… do… do… How come you do me…"
PERRY	Come in?
MAE	Oh, granny. Where did you get that fur coat?
PERRY	Come closer child, so I can look at you.
MAE	Grandma, what big eyes you got!
PERRY	(sniffing) Perfume?
MAE	Hmmm… grandma, what a big nose you have! And what teeth!
PERRY	I'm not your grandma, Little Red Riding Hood! I'm the wolf!
MAE	Well, it's about time you showed up!
PERRY	Come to my arms, my little flower of the forest.
MAE	Not so fast, wolfy!
PERRY	But we can be like Romeo and Juliet, and like Anthony and Cleopatra.
MAE	Can't we just be like Sears and Roebuck?
PERRY	No, no! Kiss me, my beauty!
	KISSING SOUND. LOUD KNOCK AT THE DOOR

MAE	Oh, shucks! Who's that?
PERRY	It's the forest ranger.
MAE	Oh, go tell him to climb a tree!
	RANGER ENTERS
RANGER	Unhand that girl, you beast!
MAE	Leave him alone!
RANGER	I'm going to shoot him!
	GUN SHOT SOUNDS
PERRY	(cries out) …aaahhhhh!
RANGER	There. I killed him!
MAE	Ya, just when things were beginning to get interesting…
RANGER	I'm sorry, honey…
MAE	Say… you're kinda cute yourself…
RANGER	Hmmm… thanks…
MAE	What are all those medals on your big strong chest?
RANGER	Well, this one is for devotion to duty. And this one is for bravery.
MAE	And this one?
RANGER	Oh. That's my good conduct medal.
MAE	Well, get rid of it, big boy, you won't be needing it anymore!

MUSIC SWELLS. FADE OUT

FINALE

PERRY   And that's the story of *Little Red Riding Hood* according to Mae West. Mae, you're just wonderful. I'm sure Mitch can sleep after that bedtime story.

MAE   Well, if he can't, he's not the man I thought he was.

PERRY   Mae, I don't know whether to ask you this or not, but have you got anything to say about Chesterfields?

MAE   Simple as A.B.C. I'll tell you why Chesterfield is my cigarette.

PERRY   Why?

MAE   Why? Because they... s – a – t – i – s – f – y...

MITCH SCREAMS OFFSTAGE, and the SOUND of a body collapsing to the floor.

PERRY   Well, there you've done it again. Mitch just fainted. Now you'll have to come back to see us again real soon. As soon as you get through with your tour of *Diamond Lil*. And lots of good luck! Goodbye, Mae West!

MAE   So long, Perry!

THE END

Mae West in *Diamond Lil,* 1950.

Mae West, 1952.

CHAPTER 4

It Ain't History, It's Herstory.

"There's nothing like a hot general in a Cold War."

ENCOURAGED BY MAE'S POSITIVE public and critical reception on *The Chesterfield Supper Club*, various producers floated ideas to present the actress on a more frequent basis on national radio. On October 7, 1950, *The Billboard* reported that "Mae West bids disc fans dial and hear her." The news item revealed the possibility of a deejay shot for Mae on WJZ, New York, in association with Charlie King. On October 14, *The Billboard* retracted the story with the headline, "Mae No Deejay!" The William Morris Agency, speaking on behalf of their client, corrected the periodical, "Tain't so, she is not associated with Charles King in any way and does not plan to do a program on the nature indicated in the news bite."

Television had shied away from the unpredictable actress for many years. West appeared for the first time on national television as a promotional stunt. The actress was in New York City, rehearsing for the February, 1949 opening of a revival of her play, *Diamond Lil*. On Sunday, December 19, 1948, she sat in the VIP audience section of *The Ed Sullivan Show* (then known as *Toast of the Town*). Sullivan introduced her from the stage. She stood up, aglow in a spotlight, to gasps from the audience, and waved, wiggled, and rolled her eyes.

Years would pass before West seriously flirted with television. In 1952, she was beginning to tire of theatrical tours. She had told a reporter in 1950 that she might be lured by a television proposal. "It will keep Dad home at least once a week," she mused. But a couple of years would pass before she conceived of a project that suited her style. Working with film director Paul H. Sloane, she developed a story originally titled *Famous Women in History*, or *Great Romances in History*. She approached her old friend, Paramount film producer, William LeBaron, to produce the show. The star and the producer talked about the project – newly titled *It Ain't History, It's Herstory* – with Walter Ames for the *Los Angeles Times*. The interview was printed on September 13, 1953.

The reporter asked the pair how they planned to get TV censors to accept the famous West figure, undulating wiggle, and suggestive delivery. Mae West wrapped a silver fox fur around her neck, and declared, "Marilyn Monroes may come and Marilyn Monroes will go but Mae West will always be the standard by which they judge sex."

LeBaron explained that they didn't intend to play up the sexy side of the legendary actress. "We're striving to make this a very funny show," he said. "We have five scripts all ready for shooting but we won't do any filming until we have at least thirteen on hand. That seems to be the most economical way to shoot television films. All the writers have instructions to go lightly on anything pertaining to love. Mae will take care of that."

Mae felt compelled to claim to be the one and only sex queen of

Hollywood. "All the new personalities coming up in the movies *try* to be sexy," she said. "They turn themselves inside out striving for recognition. Me, I don't have to do a thing to be called sexy except to stand up. Those life preservers in the Air Force named after me weren't called 'Mae Wests' for nothin'. Everyone knows I once saved Paramount studios from going bankrupt. Let's wait until some of these younger queens have broken some of my box office records before handing them my laurels."

It Ain't History, It's Herstory was set in a wax museum. Each episode would begin with a guided tour, where the host related a story surrounding the statue of an historical figure. As he began his story, the wax statue of the female character dissolved into Mae West, who proceeded to act out what she called "the real story" behind the story.

"This new television series is made to order for Mae, and will be real adult fare," LeBaron explained. "Of course, they will be completely historically inaccurate and filled with gags. As an example, in the Fatima and Bluebeard film, Mae will come to life as a private eye who gets the goods on Bluebeard for all the murders he commits.

"When Mae plays Cleopatra, the guide will tell how Caesar invades Egypt because it looks like a fat land for him to conquer. Cleo, or Mae, will be shown in our films as putting it all over poor Caesar as only a woman could. In short, it will be a crazy, mixed-up comedy of ancient history given the modern television treatment. If we can get half the scenes on television that Mae is famous for in the movies, we'll be all right."

The series was meant to cover many of history's great love affairs. Mae told the reporter that she had received many offers to work on television but turned them all down until the right vehicle showcasing her talents presented itself. She said LeBaron presented just such an idea, and the two formed their own production company to finally bring Mae West to television audiences.

Mae West at home in the Ravenswood.

She complained in the October, 1953 issue of *Theater Arts* magazine that men had written history, distorting and often dismissing the important contributions made by women in the past. She said she intended to correct that by presenting the female perspective. "These pictures will not be written from the man's point of view," she explained. "They aren't history. They are a woman's story." The shows would be comedic, but she wanted to take a swipe at a patriarchal society that had subjugated women for centuries.

Comedy writers were hired to craft script ideas for the proposed series. West and LeBaron tinkered with the several scripts presented to them. Writing and rewriting dragged on for months until the series was ultimately scrapped. The actress felt that television censorship, more stifling than the restrictions she faced during her film career, would simply preclude her from being "herself." And ultimately, no one could write for Mae West, except Mae West.

The first episode, "Mae West Meets Cleopatra," is the only remaining complete teleplay presented to LeBaron and his star. At that time, commercial spots and commercial "lead-ins" were written into the script.

INTRODUCTION

ANNOUNCER Ladies and gentlemen. This evening, (sponsor), makers of (product), take pleasure in leading you through the labyrinths of MAE WEST'S WAX WORKS. Here, you will see the mystery of history unfurled – yes, unfurled, furled, and re-furled, as you have never seen it before. But first, let us listen to a gentleman who waxes eloquent whenever he unfurls the name of (sponsor).

COMMERCIAL INSERT

SCENE: A DROP showing the entrance to MAE WEST'S WAX WORKS – with appropriate pictures of the scenes inside.

ANNOUNCER   And now, off we go into the wild, black yonder where we will witness the pains, passions, pleasures and pulchritude of the past. And when I say pulchritude, I mean the one and only lady of the wax works - MISS MAE WEST!

SCENE: THE WAX WORKS. FADE IN SLOWLY ON BLACK. THEN, FADE UP SLOWLY revealing a section of the museum. There are two conventional exhibits of wax figures. On the extreme left, perhaps Henry VIII and all his wives – next, perhaps Napoleon and Josephine – and on the extreme right, Cleopatra and Julius Caesar. Miss West is posed as Cleopatra – a guest starring actor in this episode, as Caesar. In a semicircle, behind them, are the wax figures of three or more Roman Legionnaires in full armor. CLEOPATRA is kneeling at CAESAR'S feet, a look of terror on her face – her hands raised in supplication as if she were begging Caesar for her life. CAESAR stands over CLEOPATRA, his hand outstretched in an imperious gesture, as if he were ordering her to get the hell out of his sight. A GUIDE leads a party of female sightseers on. One little henpecked guy tags along behind the women. The GUIDE is an old "carney grifter." He goes into his mechanical spiel. He's done it a thousand times and he drones on through the side of his mouth like an old phonograph record – except when he interrupts the spiel for his lousy jokes. He alone laughs at these jokes – it is part of the routine – he breaks himself up. He brings his party up close to the CAESAR and CLEOPATRA exhibit.

GUIDE   Now, ladies and gents, this here is one of the most stupendious, startling exhibits of the whole works. It was created at terrific expense by our high class staff of archeologists, anthropologists, morticians and cosmeticians who spent fifty years studying history right on the spot. Ancient Egypt and Ancient Rome. Her – that's Cleopatra, the Queen of Ancient Egypt where she lived. These figures are absolutely life-like, made of human skin and hair brought from over there. This is positively exactly the way they looked two thousand years ago – taken from authentic photographs. Now, history teaches us that two thousand years ago, they were having a cold war between Julius Caesar's Rome and Cleopatra's Egypt just exactly the same as we're having a cold war today. That just goes to show you what you all know – and that is that history repeats itself. Like a radish, you might say. (He laughs at his own joke.) Now, this great general,

Julius Caesar, had conquered every country in sight and so he started looking around for new worlds to conquer – new places to shoot off his Roman candles, you might say. (He laughs at his own joke.) And that's how come he cast his eye on Egypt, the promised land – and promised himself to move in. Business was good in Egypt – a pot for every chicken, you might say (laughs) – but they didn't have hardly any army at all. And to make it easier for Caesar, the Queen of Egypt was a woman. It looked like a pushover. So Caesar got his panzer's polished up, (He laughs at his own joke) and started out for Egypt. Now this Julius Caesar had a great army. History tells us they called armies "legions" in them days – and on the seventeenth of August, at a quarter past ten in the morning, Caesar stood at the gates of Alexandria with his great legions just itching to conquer all of Egypt. Now Cleopatra, being a woman, and not knowing anything about war, was terrified with Caesar's legionnaires right outside her palace gates. You can see her right there, on her knees, begging the great Caesar for mercy. That's taken right outta history –

GUIDEpauses while everyone in the group studies the exhibit. MAE WEST'S voice speaks out.

MAE WEST'S V.O.   History is a fake!

There is a startled HUSH. Everyone looks at everyone else. The GUIDE turns to one of the women.

GUIDE   Did you say something, Miss?

MISS   No.

GUIDE   That's funny. I thought I heard someone speaking.

MISS   So did I, but it wasn't me.

GUIDE   Any of you other ladies say anything?

They look at him in silent awe. They shake their heads. The GUIDE is puzzled.

GUIDE   I must be having a hallucination. (He shakes it off.) I keep hearing voices all the time lately.

GUIDE   (Cont.) Well, getting back to history…

MAE WEST'S V.O.   *History* is about men only. Why don't you tell them *herstory*! It's more fun!

Startled again, the GUIDE points to another one of the ladies in the party.

GUIDE   You said something, lady!

LADY   (Indignant) I did not! It was somebody else. I heard it, too.

GUIDE   It must be them clams I ate last night. (Shakes it off.) Well, getting back to history – You all know what they say about this Cleopatra – she had a kind of a bad reputation, you might say. She played around in all them night spots – like the Sphinx Club – The Pyramids – The Catacombs. Even today they say you can see the ruins of them places. But one thing she was – and that was beautiful. Not very bright – but beautiful. To use a modern colloquial expression, you might say she was beautiful but dumb –

MAE WEST'S V.O.   Any dame smart enough to be beautiful is smart enough to make it pay off.

This time, the GUIDE is really thrown. He lifts his cane, staring at the figure of Cleopatra. Then, he prods the figure as if expecting it to spring to life and jump at him. But CLEOPATRA doesn't move.

GUIDE: (Half to himself) I could have sworn I heard her talking. I guess I've been here too long. Yes, sir, when them dummies start talking back to you – you've been here too long. (Back to his spiel) Well, like I was saying – history tells us that here was the mighty Caesar, ready to conquer Egypt. And all Cleopatra could do without any army was to beg for mercy and roll her big blue eyes at him.

MAE WEST'S V.O.   Any dame with no army who can keep her country out of war must have something besides big blue eyes.

This comment really throws the GUIDE. He herds his little group together.

GUIDE   Step this way, ladies and gents – to the next stupendous exhibit and I'll show you what history tells us about George Washington, the father of his country, who never told a lie… and never tried to keep talking after he was dead.

The GUIDE leads the group away. The CAMERA moves in close to the tableau of CLEOPATRA and CAESAR. CLEOPATRA (MAE WEST) comes to life. She takes a cautious look after the GUIDE and his party – then, rises and faces full into the CAMERA.

CLEOPATRA   Now, I'll give you the real low-down. I'll show you *her* story. (She sidles up to CAESAR who has not moved from his original position. She looks him in the eye for a long moment. Then, suddenly, she kicks him in the shin.) Down boy! Let's get this picture right! (CAESAR drops to his knees and takes the position of supplication which CLEOPATRA held. She assumes his former pose – holding her arm, as he did, with a commanding, imperious gesture.)

The CAMERA moves forward to a CLOSE UP of CLEOPATRA as she looks into the lens and speaks.

CLEOPATRA   Why don't you come up here with me? You'll see what really happened when Caesar came to conquer Egypt.

DISSOLVE INTO:

SCENE: A richly overdressed boudoir-sitting room. Outside entrance is up stage center. Inside entrances left and right. Ornate furniture; chaise lounges, love seats, couches, floor cushions – all appropriate to the playing of intimate scenes. For each episode, there will be a slight change in the decorative dressing of the set, in keeping with the episode's time in history. On the right wall there is a huge, built-in commode which, when opened, will reveal plot-props for use in all the various episodes. At the moment, the decorative motif of the set is Egyptian. On a pedestal there is a bust of an Egyptian pharaoh.

CLEOPATRA is discovered, seductively gracing a chaise lounge. Her BUTLER enters. He is dressed very formally in full livery. He wears an Egyptian headdress. His headdress will change with the period of each episode. He is very British – very elegant. He addresses his Queen.

BUTLER Pardon your Majesty.

CLEOPATRA What is it, Shanks?

BUTLER The general is here.

CLEOPATRA Which general? Incoming or outgoing?

BUTLER General Julius Caesar, Majesty.

CLEOPATRA Oh, him. What's he like? How does he look?

BUTLER   Hot, Madam. Hot under the collar. That's just a figure of speech, of course. He hasn't got any collar. But if he had one – he'd look hot under it.

CLEOPATRA   That's good. Keep him that way. There's nothing like a hot general in a cold war. Give him a drink – but take the ice cubes away.

BUTLER   Yes, Madam.

CLEOPATRA   And when you show him in – tell him to hold the fort. I'll just slip into my – chariot – and be right over.

BUTLER   Very good, Madam. (He turns and begins to leave.)

CLEOPATRA   (calls him back) Oh, Shanks! (She points to the bust of Pharaoh on the pedestal.) Set Julius up in the main alley.

BUTLER   Very good, Madam.

                CLEOPATRA exits to the left. The BUTLER takes the statue of the Pharaoh from the pedestal and moves to the commode, or huge closet stage right. As he opens the doors we see a collection of busts and paintings and props which are to be used in future scenes – everything from Napoleon the First to Mary the Frigid. He puts the Pharaoh's bust away – finds the bust of Caesar – blows the dust off it and sets it on the pedestal. Then he moves to the door upstage to admit JULIUS CAESAR.

BUTLER	Won't you come in, General? Her Majesty will audience you in just a moment.
CAESAR	(Storms into the room – in full armor – burning mad.) She's kept me waiting!
BUTLER	Yes, General.
CAESAR	I don't allow *anybody* to keep me waiting! Your Queen will pay for this!
BUTLER	Yes, General.
CAESAR	I'm Julius Caesar! *The* Julius Caesar!
BUTLER	Yes, General. May I take your crown?
CAESAR	No!
BUTLER	Yes, General. May I fix you a drink?
CAESAR	No!
BUTLER	Yes, General. Won't you…
CAESAR	No!
BUTLER	Yes, General. (The BUTLER exits right, taking the ice bucket with him. CAESAR yells after him.)
CAESAR	I've got a good mind to order the attack right this minute. Who does this Cleopatra think *she* is? Doesn't she know who *I* am?
	OFFSTAGE a fanfare of bugles and a ruffle of drums. CLEOPATRA enters in the doorway at left.

CLEOPATRA   Yes, General.

CAESAR   (Whirls to face her. He gapes at her.) Who are you?

CLEOPATRA   Want to guess? It starts with "C" – and you never can tell how it'll end.

>   CLEOPATRA flicks the light switch at the door. The set goes dark, except for a spot which bathes her in light. Another spot lights CAESAR. For the rest, only the few Egyptian decorations are seen in soft light. We'll get our atmosphere in each episode with lighting – and a few, period props. Wherever CLEOPATRA moves, the spot follows. Same with CAESAR and other characters.

CAESAR   You are – you are the Queen? Cleopatra? (He keeps staring at her.)

CLEOPATRA   See anything you like? (Caesar doesn't answer. Just stares.) All right. You guessed me. Now, let me guess you.

CAESAR   (Keeps gaping – snaps out of it.) No! I've got no time for games. I've got umpteen thousand Legionnaires out there at your gates, champing at the bit.

>   Another FANFARE of bugles and drums. The BUTLER shows a MESSENGER in. The MESSENGER wears Roman armor – and an American Legion cap – carries a bugle.

MESSENGER General, the men are champing at the bit.

CLEOPATRA He just said that.

MESSENGER Pardon, Ma'am. But our men refuse to wait any longer. They want to attack.

CAESAR (To Cleopatra) That's your fault! You can't keep Legionnaires waiting, you know. Not those boys!

CLEOPATRA I can keep any boys waiting – as long as they're boys! Tell them to hold their horses. It might be worth their while.

CAESAR (Her reading of that line gets him – he goes soft.) Say – where have you been all – (catches himself – goes hard again.) – where have you been all this time?

CLEOPATRA I was searching all over the palace. I couldn't find the bubbles for my bath. You'll have to excuse me.

CAESAR No!

CLEOPATRA (moves toward Caesar) Won't you... sit down?

CAESAR No! And *no* to everything else! I can see you like only *yes* men around you!

CLEOPATRA Oh... I try to keep the place sociable.

CAESAR Well, here's one man who won't *yes* you. I'll *no* you, and *no* you until...

CLEOPATRA Good. I'd like to know you, too.

Another insistent FANFARE from off stage.

MESSENGER (Holding the bugle ready.) General… shall I blow the call to attack?

CLEOPATRA (to Messenger) You heard him, son. He says no to everything. Don't blow attack. Just blow off.

MESSENGER Yes, your Majesty.

CLEOPATRA You're a smart kid. Tell those Legionnaires I'll see them later. Maybe we'll have a convention.

MESSENGER Yes, your Majesty. (He exits.)

CAESAR I want you to know that my calling on you is only a matter of courtesy.

CLEOPATRA Thanks. I'll be glad to return the courtesy. Why don't you go back to Rome and let me come up and see *you* sometime?

CAESAR Oh, no, you don't. I've read all about you. I know what you did to Mark Antony.

CLEOPATRA That hasn't happened yet, General. He comes *after* you.

CAESAR Oh? Well anyway, I came here to conquer Egypt – and conquer I will. Veni. Vidi. Vici. I came. I saw. I conquered. Someday I'm going to say that. Why, I could crush your country as easily as that. (He snaps his fingers – loud.)

CLEOPATRA That's quite a snap you've got, General. Do you do everything (snaps her fingers) that easy?

CAESAR	Everything. But I'm too much of a gentleman to subjugate Egypt before giving you a chance to surrender – without resistance.
CLEOPATRA	Not even – a *little* resistance, General?
CAESAR	No!
CLEOPATRA	But this is so sudden. We've only just met. You haven't even taken off your crown. (Embarrassed, CAESAR takes off his crown.) You've got to give me a little time.
CAESAR	There is no time! Tempus fugit!
CLEOPATRA	But I've got to talk to my army. Why, that whole army leans on me.
CAESAR	Army? You haven't got any army. It's a joke.
CLEOPATRA	Well, I like a little joke once in a while. Have you heard any good ones lately?
CAESAR	No! Now, for the last time – will you surrender quietly? Or shall I turn my legions loose on Egypt?
CLEOPATRA	When you put it that way, Julius, what else can I do? For my country – anything!
CAESAR	For a woman, you show good sense. I'll tell you my terms.
CLEOPATRA	I know, Julius. So much down – and so much a week. I got my palace that way.
	FANFARE – bugles and drums. The BUTLER shows the MESSENGER in.

MESSENGER   General, the men are champing – I mean we can't hold them any longer. They're getting hungry – and you told them Egypt was full of goodies.

CAESAR   Tell them that Caesar has taken Egypt without a shot. There will be feasting tonight. The Queen is surrendering!

MESSENGER   Yes, General. (MESSENGER exits.)

CLEOPATRA   (calls after the Butler) Oh, Shanks!

BUTLER   Yes, your Majesty?

CLEOPATRA   While I'm surrendering, see what the boys at the back gate will have. And – set *two* plates for dinner.

BUTLER   Yes, your Majesty. (BUTLER exits.)

CLEOPATRA moves to the pedestal on which Caesar's bust stands. Her movements are very deliberate – planned. CAESAR's eyes follow her and, for the first time, he notices the statue. CLEOPATRA gazes at the statue, in adoration. Now, she starts to put on the act for CAESAR.

CAESAR   What's that?

CLEOPATRA   (very dramatic) That's the statue of the man I've worshipped all my life. My *only* love. It has never been moved off that pedestal. Ever since I was a little girl he has been my idol… my ideal!

CAESAR   He *has*?!

CLEOPATRA   He has! He holds the place of honor in my heart and in the hearts of all my countrymen! Why, when I go to bed at night, they move the statue right into the royal bedchamber. It is the last thing my eyes gaze on at night – the first thing they see with the rising sun.

CAESAR   (He sounds like Elmer Snerd.) No-o-o-o-o-...

CLEOPATRA   Yes!

CAESAR   But that's me!

CLEOPATRA   You? General, I wouldn't breathe your name in the same breath as his. That man – is Julius Caesar!

CAESAR   But that's me – that's I – that's me, I tell you! (He isn't quite sure of the grammar.) I'm Julius Caesar – can't you see it in my eyes?!

CLEOPATRA   Your eyes are bloodshot and shifty. His are bright and noble, even in the cold, cold marble. Do you think the great, the wonderful, the God-like Caesar would make war on a defenseless woman? Do you think that Julius Caesar would bring umpteen thousand Legionnaires to Cleopatra's home – like it was a Convention Hall – champing at the bit, yet – and order the Queen Cleopatra to surrender or else? Like Capone? (CAESAR tries to speak, but she continues.) The answer is No! A thousand times, No! And tell all your friends I said, No! Because Julius Caesar is the greatest general in the world – the noblest Roman of them all. A true soldier among men – a true gentleman among women!

CAESAR But…

CLEOPATRA But me no buts. If the mighty Caesar came here at all it would be because he wanted to protect me. Because he knows that women weren't made for fighting. They were made for… finer things.

CAESAR Your Majesty… maybe we ought to talk this over.

CLEOPATRA Over what? Before we do any… talking… let me see your identification.

CAESAR (Takes a card out and hands it to Cleopatra.) My driver's license.

CLEOPATRA (She compares the picture on the license with the face of the bust and with CAESAR's features.)

Well! If you had a feather, you could knock me over! (She turns to address the statue.) Oh, glorious Caesar, why did you do this to me? Why did you let me go on loving you so long? And now, you turn out to be… (She wheels about and points a finger under CAESAR's nose.) THIS! A woman fighter! A bully! A mobster! Oh, how the mighty have fallen!

CAESAR   Your Majesty – you haven't met the real me. I'll admit that sometimes I'm a bit hasty – impetuous, you might even say. But underneath this hard exterior, there's a bright, flaming jewel in Julius.

CLEOPATRA   I always dreamed that Caesar and I would rule together – in peace. The USCC. United States of Cleopatra and Caesar! One empire! Rome in the west – Egypt in the east. I dreamed that we'd play East-West games in the Rose Bowl. That Caesar would be greater than just great – because he finally knew the love of a good woman! But it's all over now. I surrender!

CAESAR   But it isn't all over! Why that's what I've wanted all my life – more than glory or empire. The love of a good woman! Look, your Majesty! Can't you see it in my eyes?!

CLEOPATRA   Come over here in the light. (She looks deep into his eyes. The old routine. Squire Smathers looking into the eyes of his wayward daughter, Nell – looking – searching – for the truth. Cleopatra looks long and deep. A big smile grows on her face.) Why, Julius! You rascal!

CAESAR   I told you! I told you! Could you see the *real* me? The jewel in Julius?

CLEOPATRA   *Could* I! Brother!

CAESAR   (Grabs CLEOPATRA in his arms.) Cleopatra, my darling! My queen!

CLEOPATRA   Julius! My… (he squeezes her too hard)… goodness!

CAESAR   I came to conquer – but I'll stay to worship. I don't care how long it takes before I get back to Rome. Years and years.

CLEOPATRA   (crafty and practical) But Julius! How about your Legionnaires? Thousands of them.

CAESAR   Let them take care of themselves. They're big boys now.

CLEOPATRA   That's what I'm afraid of. It would be like a buffalo stampede all over Egypt. Ah, my Julius, I can see that you need more than the love of a good woman.

CAESAR   You mean there's *more*?!

CLEOPATRA   Yes. Brains.

CAESAR   (let down) Oh, *that*.

CLEOPATRA   What's going to happen to Rome while you're basking on the Nile?

CAESAR   Happen? Nothing. My friends are taking care of Rome while I'm away.

CLEOPATRA   What friends?

CAESAR   Why, all of them. Brutus, Cassius, Casca…

CLEOPATRA   You haven't got any friends in Rome!

CAESAR   That's ridiculous!

CLEOPATRA	No, it isn't. They let you go out and fight all the wars and sow the glory for Rome – but *they* reap it. They've been playing you for a sucker, Julius. You've been all over the world fighting for years. And they've been plotting to take Rome away from you.
CAESAR	I don't believe it! They're my friends, I tell you!
CLEOPATRA	Okay. Listen to this.
	CLEOPATRA takes a tape recorder out of a drawer and turns it on. The tape plays. Angry voices are heard. The following dialogue between CAESAR and CLEOPATRA is spoken over the voices on the tape. CLEOPATRA and CAESAR listen just long enough to get the gist of the speeches, but their own action is not delayed. The tape just plays until it runs out.
CASSIUS V.O.	(Voice on the tape recorder.) Now in the names of all the Gods at once, upon what meat doth this our Caesar feed, that he is grown so great? Rome – thou art shamed. Rome – thou hast lost the breed of noble bloods.
CLEOPATRA	Do you know that voice?
CAESAR	It's Cassius!
CLEOPATRA	Your *friend*.
BRUTUS V.O.	(Voice on the tape recorder.) But, alas, Caesar must bleed for it. Let's kill him boldly but not

	wrathfully. Let's carve him as a dish fit for the Gods.
CAESAR	That's Brutus!
CLEOPATRA	Yes. Your *best* friend. He only wants to carve you as a dish for the Gods.
	The tape continues to play in the background, but CAESAR and CLEOPATRA pay no attention.
V.O.	(Voice on the tape recorder.) Why, man, he doth bestride the narrow world, like a colossus and we petty men, walk under his huge legs and peep about, to find ourselves dishonorable graves. Men at some time are masters of their fate. The fault, dear Brutus, is not in our stars, but in ourselves that we are underlings.
CAESAR	Where did you get that recording?
CLEOPATRA	One of my friends. J. Edgar…
CAESAR	But how?!
CLEOPATRA	They told me that Brutus was plotting to take Rome away from you. So I sent my FBI down there. They planted a couple of microphones - and there you are!
CAESAR	(deeply upset) Ye Gods! My dearest friends! The dirty double crossers!
CLEOPATRA	You'd better go back to Rome, Julius. Pronto! Veni – Vidi – Vici – Vamoosi!

CAESAR   Yes! Vamoosi! I'll never forget you for this, my Queen!

CLEOPATRA   Don't mention it, Julius. Just take those Legionnaires out of here. You'll need 'em where you're goin'.

CAESAR   But I can't leave you, my darling. I told you – I need the love of a good woman – above all else.

CLEOPATRA   I'll bring it with me – above all else. You see, I just got me some community property out your way!

CAESAR   Yes, it's yours. All yours.

CLEOPATRA   Good. They say that all roads lead to Rome. Just watch for me on Highway 101.

               The MESSENGER rushes in – the BUTLER follows. FANFARE and bugles.

MESSENGER   General – the men are still champing for action.

CAESAR   Order the columns turned about! We're going to march back for the glory of the United States of Caesar and Cleopatra!

CLEOPATRA   Julius!

CAESAR   …er …of Cleopatra and Caesar!

               The MESSENGER exits. Offstage there is a tremendous blowing of bugles and beating of drums – louder and noisier than ever. The BUTLER looks on in uncomprehending amazement.

CLEOPATRA	I'll be seeing you, Julius.
CAESAR	Yes, your Majesty. I'll keep the jewel in Julius flaming bright!
	CAESAR exits with a flourish. Bugles and drums begin to recede in the background.
CLEOPATRA	Oh, Shanks!
BUTLER	Yes, your Majesty.
CLEOPATRA	Only one plate for dinner.
BUTLER	Yes, your Majesty.
CLEOPATRA	But pack my bags. I may be gone for quite a while. I'm going to do – as the Romans do.
BUTLER	(begins to leave, but stops as he finds the crown which CAESAR has forgotten and left behind.) Your Majesty. The general forgot his crown. Shall I run after him?
CLEOPATRA	No. I'll take it with me. And – if he's a good boy, I'll give it back to him.
	DISSOLVE INTO:
SCENE:	THE WAX WORKS.
	CLEOPATRA and CAESAR are discovered as we last left them – CAESAR still on his knees in supplication. The only difference is that CLEOPATRA is holding CAESAR'S crown in her hand. She looks into the camera.

CLEOPATRA   Well, that's the way Cleopatra saved Egypt. Don't tell me you couldn't use a dame like that – right here – today. So, here's the lesson I want all you girls to take away from tonight's story; You can win a cold war without firing a shot, it all depends on what *else* you've got!

GUIDE V.O.   (OFFSTAGE) Now ladies and gents, if you'll follow me, I'll show you another one of our stupendious exhibits, brought to this exhibition at tremendous cost, just so you folks can learn the true facts about history. (During this speech, the GUIDE's voice grows louder as it approaches.)

CLEOPATRA hears the GUIDE's voice approaching. She grabs hold of CAESAR and starts to pull him to his feet.

CLEOPATRA   Up boy! Here comes history!

Quickly, CAESAR and CLEOPATRA exchange places again and go back to their original poses with CLEOPATRA on her knees. In her hurry, she almost forgets to give CAESAR back his crown. He gets it back on his head just in the nick of time. The GUIDE leads the party across the set. He casts a baleful glance at CLEOPATRA, and hurries past, the little group following.

The camera pans the GUIDE and his party, past the Cleopatra and Caesar exhibit, and dollies along to the next exhibit where the party stops.

This exhibition is set up for the commercial – just as if it might be another one of the features in The Wax Works. The GUIDE can lead into the commercial and let one of the "wax figures" come to life for the body of the commercial. This setting will lend itself to the clever selling of any product whether it be cigarettes, beer or automobiles. At the end of commercial, dissolve to the Back Drop showing the entrance to MAE WEST'S WAX WORKS.

ANNOUNCER V.O. Come visit us at the Wax Works next week, won't you, when Mae West will once again set the record straight with another classic from *herstory*.

FADE OUT

THE END

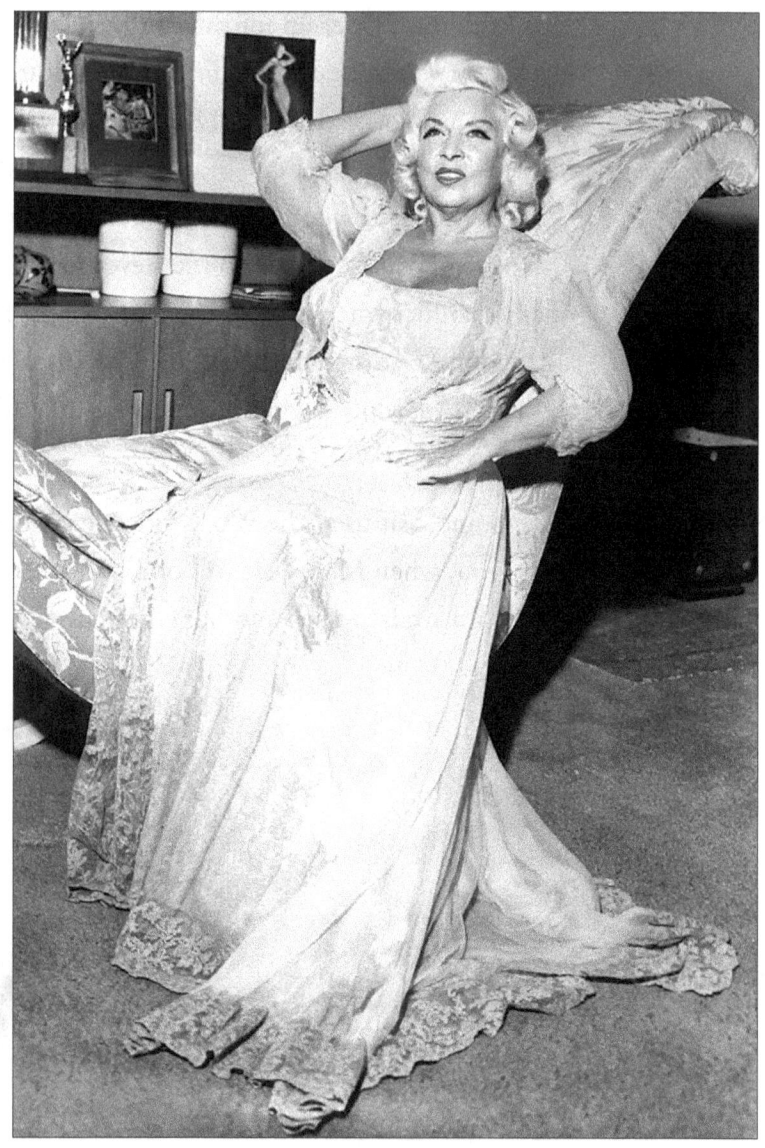

Mae West at her Santa Monica beach house, 1954.

CHAPTER 5

Mae West meets Oscar, and *The Mae West Show*

"There's certainly nothing wrong with a plumber. Of course, it's better if he has the right pipes, nuts and U-joints."

THE ACTRESS'S LONGTIME MANAGER, lawyer and friend, James A. Timony suffered a heart attack and died at his Los Angeles home on April 5, 1954. He had been ill for several years, and lived in a bungalow behind a playhouse he managed at 1743 North New Hampshire Avenue. Mae felt the loss deeply. Timony's death would prove to be a game changer for his sole, world-famous client. Their plans to build a casino to be named, "Diamond Lil's," on property Mae purchased in Las Vegas were scuttled, but she proceeded with a nightclub act they concocted – starring the actress and featuring a chorus line of scantily clad, record-holding musclemen – which premiered at the Sahara Hotel in Las Vegas on July 27, 1954. "Mae West and Her Adonises," a smash hit, toured the United States for one year.

Mae and Rock Hudson posing at the base of a giant Oscar statue at the Pantages Theater in Hollywood, 1958.

Decca Records released West's LP, *The Fabulous Mae West*, in 1956 which featured some of the songs from her nightclub act. The record was a big seller, and a critical success. Her stage show played return engagements in April through June, and then Mae embarked on a summer stock tour in the play, *Come on Up, Ring Twice*. She then settled into her Ravenswood apartment to begin work on her autobiography with the assistance of author Stephen Longstreet and her long-time secretary, Larry Lee.

On July 11, 1956, she told reporter William Peper that she was contemplating film and television offers. She reminisced about her box office appeal, which saved Paramount from bankruptcy, and joked that if she did appear on television the powers that be would not make her stand still, "the way they did to Elvis Presley," on *The Steve Allen Plymouth Show* several days earlier.

"But I don't know whether I'll get my own way," she remarked. "They don't need to be rescued yet. TV is doin' pretty good at the moment, and they're tryin' to cramp m'style. Why they practically want to put me in a Mother Hubbard and dark glasses. But I won't do it that way. I got to move around. This is the way I'm at m'best."

Two months later, *The New York Post* printed an interview with Mae on September 2. The actress told the reporter, Frances Herridge, that she hoped to make her television debut in a specially produced spectacular of her play, *Diamond Lil*, if she could circumvent the censors. Characters and plot lines were modified by the actress to appease the censors, including changing the nationality of villainous characters from Hispanic to Russian, and abandoning the white slavery storyline in favor of a counterfeiting ring. "A couple of men – six of 'em in fact, were up talking to me about it the other night," she explained. "But I gotta see if they'll let me do it my way. I never disappoint my audience." She said she had received many television offers, but rejected the scripts. "It's got to be special for my personality. That's why I always write my own stuff, like Chaplin."

Work slowly progressed on her autobiography, but she finally accepted an offer to appear on television that was too enticing to turn down. Producer Jerry Wald had been engaged to produce the 30th Academy Awards ceremony to be broadcast live on NBC-TV on March 26, 1958. More than 70 of the biggest stars in Hollywood were scheduled to participate. Wald wanted Mae to sing "Baby, It's Cold Outside" with Rock Hudson in a large, musical production. The idea to team West and Hudson was an intriguing one. Both stars had recently battled *Confidential Magazine* over slanderous stories. The actress had been accused of sleeping with one of her former Black employees, and the magazine had threatened to "out" leading man, Rock Hudson, the number one male box office attraction. To pair the two was a none-too-subtle jab at the dreaded gossip magazine.

Rock Hudson and Mae rehearse for the 1958 Oscar Awards.

Jerry called Mae personally to ask her to appear on the show. Mae recalled, "He said, 'It is estimated that ninety million will be watching.' I said, ninety million what?" With a potential audience that big, she thought this would be the perfect way to make her television debut.

Rock and Mae rehearse.

Her acceptance of the offer did not come without certain caveats, however. She required control of her stage costume, private rehearsal time, and the right to write her own material. Mae said, I told Jerry, "there have to be changes to the lyrics of 'Baby, It's Cold Outside,' to adapt them to my particular personality and style of delivery." The producer acquiesced. The day before the telecast, Mae called her friend, and designer of choice, Edith Head, who was coordinating the wardrobe for the show. She told Edith she would not be wearing a black and white fitted sheath as planned, but another, more eye-catching Head design.

Mae and Rock privately rehearsed at her apartment for several days with a pianist, and a song writer named Charles Henderson. "We gradually got 'Baby, It's Cold Outside' real cool in a hot way," she recalled.

The official briefing session with the entire performing cast took place on Sunday, March 23. Monday and Tuesday preceding the broadcast, rehearsals were conducted at the RKO Pantages Theater on Hollywood Boulevard, the site of the ceremony.

Rock and Mae at the Oscars.

At a cost of $850,000, the Motion Picture Academy, with the financial assistance of producer Mike Todd (who died in a plane crash, days before the show), broadcast the three-and-a-half-hour spectacle without commercial interruption. Bob Hope, Rosalind Russell, David Niven, James Stewart, Jack Lemmon, and Donald Duck traded hosting duties. More than seventy major film stars participated in the ceremony.

The show had a story line – the past, present and future of Hollywood. Twenty-one stars performed in the opening musical production number, which consisted of a medley of past Academy Award winning songs. Marge and Gower Champion danced "The Continental," and the singers included Tony Martin, Betty Grable, Rhonda Fleming, Bob Hope, Van Johnson, Mae and Rock. On March 27, Thomas M. Pryor wrote in *The New York Times*, "Miss West and Mr. Hudson stole this interlude, if not the entire show with their suggestive singing of 'Baby, It's Cold Outside.'"

With a set consisting of a single decorative chaise longue, Mae West wiggled, undulated, plumped her blond hair, pursed her lips and rolled her eyes to wild cheers from the audience. She was resplendent in a form-fitting, black sequined gown trimmed in yards of white fox fur, and a feathered headdress. When the number began, Rock Hudson reclined on the chaise, hidden from the audience – only his legs protruding from behind the actress. When he suddenly sat up revealing himself, the audience roared. Rock held Mae in his arms while they sang, and midway through the number, offered her a cigarette, saying, "King-sized." She purred, "hmmmm," but quickly tossed it over her head. The short number was not flawless. They stepped on each other's lines near the end, but quickly recovered to canoodle. Mae ended the performance with a signature line, "Oh, like I always say, it's not the men in your life that counts, it's the life in your men."

Rock and Mae perform live on the Oscar show.

She recalled, "Oscar events are usually very stuffy. I unstuffed this one. I brought it out of the clouds of unreal rehearsed humility, and down to one man and a woman."

Reviews of the spectacle were mixed. *Daily Variety*, usually critical of the broadcast, thought the show was memorable, "one that will serve as a notable model for others to come." On one thing, critics did agree – Mae West was a hit!

Philip K. Scheuer wrote in the *Los Angeles Times* on March 27,

"Last evening's turnout was the most glamorous and spectacular in many years. One had to go clear back to the era of silent films at their peak to find a comparable assemblage of names – and those were days in which Hollywood was one compact colony. It was such a program as could bring together such hilarious opposites as Mae West and Rock Hudson dueting in 'Baby, It's Cold Outside.' The indestructible Miss West received a tremendous hand at her entrance."

The *Los Angeles Herald Examiner* headlined, "MAE WEST, ROCK, STOP OSCAR SHOW." They wrote, "Mae West and Rock Hudson stopped the show cold! Mae, appearing in a black sequined gown, white fur and a white plume headdress, and singing, 'Baby, It's Cold Outside" with Rock, brought down the house!"

Mae immodestly stated, "I was a hit on the newest thing in show business – television – with my own trademark, a man in my arms. My phone never stopped ringing for three days, and a snowstorm of letters and telegrams descended on me. I became aware that I was, whether I liked it or not, an institution."

Mae's show-stopping appearance on the Oscar special generated renewed interest in finding a television vehicle for her. Many ideas were contemplated. Of particular note, three different treatments were prepared for a television series. *Portrait of a Lady: An Original Story Written for Mae West*, and *The Lady and the Lawman: An Original Story Written for Mae West* were credited to a writer named Dahl Lee Lyons – a pseudonym for Dolly Lyons Dempsey. Dolly was a lifetime fan and friend of the actress, and the president of her first official fan club. The third treatment, which was untitled, was the most fully developed. It concerned a blonde singer, described as a "sex goddess" named Glory Carter, who abandons the comfort of New York City for the Wild West. The episodes involved her exploits in the uncharted west, with the many rough and tumble characters along the way. The story began on a train headed to Gold City where Glory would perform at the notorious Golden Bar Saloon. The train is robbed on route, and upon arrival at the station in Gold City, the passengers are questioned about the crime by the handsome sheriff. Glory sizes up the sheriff, and says, "Hmmm…any more like you at home?" The sheriff replies, "Yes, ma'm, six brothers, and we're really alike." Glory answers, "Mmmm…one for every day of the week."

No scripts were ever completed.

On August 21, 1958, *Variety* reported a Mae West TV series in the works. Actor Steve Cochran's company, Robert Alexander Productions, floated the idea of a series titled, *Klondike Lil*. Mae would play an "adventuress" in the gold country of Alaska. Robert Schwartz and Cochran would co-produce the show. Robert Stevens worked on a pilot script to be directed by Cochran – who would co-star with the actress. Steve Cochran had starred with West in the 1949 Broadway revival of her play, *Diamond Lil*. Ambitious plans called for location filming in Dawson, Alaska. As the months waned, the series was abandoned in favor of a motion picture, but ultimately nothing was ever filmed.

Mae was also presented with a proposal for a half-hour series set in her Hollywood apartment titled, *Come Up and See Me Sometime*. More than a dozen short "tease" scripts were prepared, but the writer is unknown. The titles include *Mae West Meets Hercules, Mae West and Santa Claus, Mae West and Durante, Mae West and the Astrologer, Mae West and King Edward, Mae West and Paladin*, and *Mae West and Matt Drillen* (a take-off on the Matt Dillon character on *Gunsmoke*). The premise was simple. The guest arrived for a visit and was ushered into her lavish apartment by her maid or Japanese houseboy named Itchi. Only a couple of script drafts remain.

Mae West and Walter Winchell

MAE	(goes to her front door) Hello, Walter. Come on in. Don't just stand there lookin' through my key hole.
WALTER	All in a day's work, Mae. Thought I could get a line on your latest heart-throb.
MAE	Yeah? I'd like to get a line on him myself.
WALTER	Now don't try to keep anything from me – speak freely.
MAE	I can't. My agent wants his ten percent.
WALTER	What's all these rumors I get about you going to be married?
MAE	If I were you, I wouldn't take in rumors.
WALTER	I had it from my girl Friday. And she's usually right.
MAE	Well, I had a man Sunday, and let him go on Monday.
WALTER	What's this I hear about you writing a book on the art of making love?
MAE	No, it's on the love of making Art.
WALTER	How's your correspondence these days?

MAE	Scorching.
WALTER	I mean, you get a lot of letters don't you?
MAE	Oh, a hundred thousand a week.
WALTER	Hmmm. I get five hundred thousand myself.
MAE	Yeah, but mine are fan letters.
WALTER	I see. I left myself wide open, didn't I?
MAE	Well, you know, anything for a laugh, Walter. What do you say? Would you like a little drink of something?
WALTER	Well, I'll take a little tomato juice for a pickup.
MAE	Fine. What'll you have for yourself? (calls out) Oh, Itchi!
ITCHI	Yes, Missy.
MAE	Be a dear. Squeeze a couple of tomatoes for Mr. Winchell.
ITCHI	Oh, Mr. Winchell, you light me up in your column and I cook you up some suki yaki.
WALTER	Are you trying to bribe me?
MAE	(laughs) The boy's got a wonderful sense of humor. He's liable to be back in a flash with a hash.
WALTER	Ah. You do read my column.
MAE	No. But I've had my attention called to it.

WALTER	Confidentially, Mae, haven't you any secrets, any skeletons in your closet that I can dig out?
MAE	Who do you take me for, Bluebeard?
WALTER	Well, tell me something I can print. For instance, do you make a practice of kissing?
MAE	Say, do you think I need any practice? By the way, what did you come up here for?

Mae West and George Bernard Shaw

The sound of loud knocking at the front door.

MAE	Sounds like someone trying to break in. Itchi, look out the door carefully.
ITCHI	I look see, Missy.

More loud knocking.

MAE	Who is it?
ITCHI	Man with long white hair on honorable chin.
SHAW (V.O.)	Are you going to let me in, you rascal? I'm Shaw! *The* Shaw!
MAE	Oh, Shaw…whiskers and all…I get it. I heard he was in Hollywood. Let him in.

Door opens and SHAW enters.

SHAW	At last! Well, Madam, this is hardly the welcome I should have expected.

MAE	Why didn't you let me know you were coming? I'd 've had a brass band.
SHAW	I detest brass bands. Besides, I never let anyone know I'm coming. I just drop in.
MAE	You should have dropped in long ago.
SHAW	This place is as difficult to get into as Buckingham Palace!
MAE	Yeah. Like one of your books, honey.
SHAW	Tush…my books are what they are. And I am what I am.
MAE	Well sit yourself down and be yourself.
SHAW	I prefer to lean on a fireplace. Have you one?
MAE	Not here. But you can try the incinerator.
SHAW	America has no culture.
MAE	When it's as old as you are, it will have.
SHAW	The compliment is well received.
MAE	I hear you're bicycling around the world, or something.
SHAW	Nothing quite as tedious. I'm motoring.
MAE	How do you like Hollywood?
SHAW	Not nearly as much as Hollywood likes me.
MAE	That must be awful. You've been around the studios, I suppose.

SHAW	Ad nauseam. And I can't understand why they need such big buildings to make such small pictures.
MAE	For the same reason that elephants are scared of mice.
SHAW	Ha, Ha! Very good! Excellent! But what does it mean?
MAE	You tell me. You're supposed to be the Sage of Adelphi Terrace.
SHAW	By the way, did I say why I came up to see you?
MAE	I don't think you mentioned it.
SHAW	Well, you have an unusual personality like myself.
MAE	Nice of you to admit it.
SHAW	Your plays, too, interest me. They are full of wit, but no technique.
MAE	And yours are full of technique. Say, how about putting down your umbrella and taking off your rubbers. This is California.
SHAW	Haven't you heard? I'm a pessimist.
MAE	Do you have to be?
SHAW	I make my living at it.
MAE	Kind of a trademark, huh? I've also heard you're a vegetarian. Live on fruits and nuts.

SHAW	Oh, yes. And carrots and potatoes. That sort of thing.
MAE	Yeah? Well, I must be practically a vegetarian myself.
SHAW	Really?
MAE	Sure. I always eat lots of potatoes with my filet mignon.

The third script offered an intriguing meeting between Mae and Will Hays, the infamous movie censor, who was her nemesis throughout her film career. It's a humorous sendup of the ridiculous nature of censorship, and expresses her feelings about the issue in typical Mae West fashion.

Mae West and Will Hays

ITCHI ushers WILL HAYS, the feared movie censor, into Mae's living room.

ITCHI	You like sit down, please? Missy in bed. She come light out an' see you.
HAYS	Huh? But she can't do that, it's against the regulations of censorship!
ITCHI	Tha' what you sinks.
MAE	(enters) Why, Itchi, I'm surprised at you talking that way to Mr. Hays.
ITCHI	He surprise, too.

MAE	Go away, now. I'll ring if I need you. How are you, Mr. Hays? Sorry if I've kept you waiting, but I thought you'd prefer it if I appeared in something less censorable than a night gown.
HAYS	Thank you. I do prefer it.
ITCHI	(lingering) Missy? Shall I pull down shades, please?
MAE	Yes. No. Go away, Itchi. Polish the silver or something. Pardon the interruption, Mr. Hays. You were saying?
HAYS	Well, to put it briefly. I came to discuss with you certain problems.
MAE	Problems? I don't have any.
HAYS	I think we all have. But I'm speaking of problems of censorship in connection with your pictures.
MAE	Oh, yes. I remember you did a little cutting on a couple of them. I handed you a script and you gave me back a bunch of confetti. Nice job.
HAYS	I'm sorry, but it has been agreed that certain rules must prevail in censoring motion picture material.
MAE	Who agreed? I didn't. And neither did a few million others.
HAYS	Nevertheless. There is a number of things one cannot say and must not do in pictures.
MAE	Yeah, I found that out. Don't get me wrong. I'll admit there's a limit to everything.

HAYS	Now that's very sensible.
MAE	Sure it is. So there ought to be a limit to censorship.
HAYS	I don't think I quite follow that thought.
MAE	Well, in plain words, what we need are censors to censor the censors. And then some more censors to censor the censors who censor the censors. Get the idea? Build it up that way until the whole thing collapses from sheer boredom and a top-heavy payroll.
HAYS	You're not serious!
MAE	I've never been more serious, and felt funnier in my life.
HAYS	At the moment, I'm concerned with the script of your new story.
MAE	What? Why the thing's positively wholesome. In spots.
HAYS	Let's consider the situation in which Calico Jenny is lying in bed eating Grape-Nuts.
MAE	Now what's the matter with Grape-Nuts?!
HAYS	It isn't the Grape-Nuts. It's the…er…mise en scene.
MAE	You mean the bed?
HAYS	Quite so! That's out – but definitely!

MAE	Why it's a marvelous scene – and when you get a sound track on it – terrific!
HAYS	Well, if it's vital to the story that the character eat Grape-Nuts, she will have to do so on some other article of furniture.
MAE	How about a chaise longue?
HAYS	No. She can't recline that much! It will have to be a chair!
MAE	Terrible. Spoils everything. Forget it. I'll stand her up in the archway. It'll make a pretty shot from Louis' angle when he first sees her.
HAYS	By the way. You can't call Louis a rat.
MAE	But he is a rat. He croaks his own brother, don't he?
HAYS	And that's another thing. He can't croak – I mean slay his own brother. That's fratricide. That's very bad.
MAE	Sure it is. That's why I say he's a rat.
HAYS	Well, if he has to kill a relative, it can't be any closer than a fourth cousin.
MAE	Then we'll skip it. I'll have him kill himself in the end.
HAYS	That's suicide. You know we don't allow that except in pictures of murder mysteries.
MAE	How about calling him a louse?
HAYS	No. We've finally banned that word.

MAE	Bum?
HAYS	No. It has a different meaning in England.
MAE	It would.
HAYS	Anyway, I suggest you don't make Louis a gangster, and I wouldn't call him Louis. It sounds foreign, and some countries might take offense.
MAE	Hmmm..is that so? I had no idea people were so broad-minded.
HAYS	In any case, you'll have to change Calico Jenny to another name. It's too – er – well suggestive of the sinister.
MAE	Too sinister, huh? Well, I'll tell you what I'll do Mr. Hays. I'll cooperate with you – I won't make Louis a gangster. I'll make him a censor, and Calico Jenny will be called Nice Nellie, a writer. And this censor comes up to see Nellie to tell her how to not write a story for the pictures, and so Nice Nellie – who was very nice up to this point – picks up a forty-five which her bodyguard had left lying around careless like, and she shoots this censor without the slightest hesitation…and he…
	(The sound of the front door loudly slamming)
MAE	(cont.) Goodness. I wonder why Mr. Hays left in such a hurry?

Mae's agent presented a number of TV comedy writers for her to consider. They finally agreed on an idea for a fifteen-minute, five-days-a-week show that presented the actress doling out advice to the lovelorn – answering letters addressed to her in care of the station. The idea was floated in the syndication market. The program would be called, *The Mae West Show*, or *Mae West Tells All About Love*. Mae was busy working on her autobiography, and allowed the writers to present pilot episodes for her review. KCOP, a local Los Angeles television station, expressed an interest in partnering with the actress, but ultimately, negotiations came to nothing, and the idea, probably too daring for the conservative 1950s, was shelved. It was again apparent that no one could effectively write for Mae West but the actress herself.

In both of the teleplays offered to her, the sets were designed to look like her real life residence. Using *The George Burns and Gracie Allen Show*, a popular situation comedy at the time, as a reference, Mae was allowed to break the "fourth wall" by communicating directly with the viewers with a nod to the camera, a wink, or an aside.

THE MAE WEST SHOW

FADE IN: (DAY)

MEDIUM SHOT: LESTER is seated on a straight chair beside and above a chaise in a lavishly decorated white and gold living room. He is a very handsome, young man with a body builder physique, with his muscles bulging in a tight t-shirt. He has a pad open on his knees, ready to take notes, though Miss West has not yet arrived. The THEME MUSIC FADES OUT and LESTER glances at his watch. He places the pad on a table and wanders around the room. He starts to sit in a chair beside a desk, but rises quickly as he realizes he is sitting on a small lace pillow. The O.S. SOUND of a door opening is heard. LESTER hurries back to his chair, picks up the pad and pencil and glances o.s. toward the bedroom door, C.R.

FULL SHOT: MAE WEST. With the door partly open, MAE WEST starts to enter, lower half of her torso first. She pauses as though her shoulders were being held back, leaving only the legs, hips, and one fur-draped arm visible. What we do see looks tremendously sexy in a revealing negligee.

MEDIUM CLOSE SHOT: LESTER reacts with shy embarrassment and occupies himself with the pad and pencil.

MEDIUM FULL SHOT: MAE WEST, still only partly visible; we hear her murmur as though saying goodbye.

MAE Do come again…

There is a pause as though her guest was whispering something.

MAE (soft, sexy) Ummm… delightful… ummmm… delicious…

MAE enters, closes the door and crosses to LES-

	TER, the picture of contentment.
MAE	Sorry. I was… De-layed…

MEDIUM SHOT: MAE and LESTER

MAE arranges herself on the chaise feeling luxuriously lazy.

LESTER	That's all right. How was your lunch with George?
MAE	Great!

CLOSE SHOT: MAE

MAE looks over her shoulder INTO CAMERA and addresses the audience.

MAE	I've never seen a man eat so much lunch!

MEDIUM SHOT: MAE and LESTER

LESTER picks up a pile of letters as MAE turns back toward him.

MAE	What's in the mail today, Lester?
LESTER	There's a letter from… (noticing her bare legs). Shall I get a cover? You might get chilly?
MAE	Honey, not for hours!
LESTER	Well, if you want it later, I'll give it to you.

CLOSE SHOT: MAE

MAE interprets this as having a double meaning. SHE turns for a quick look INTO CAMERA, and rolls her eyes.

MEDIUM CLOSE SHOT: MAE and LESTER

MAE studies LESTER carefully, mentally taking him into the bedroom. He looks good.

MAE: I might like it…

LESTER: Then I'll get it…

MAE: Sit down, honey. Get on with the mail.

LESTER eases back into the chair, shaking his head over the inconsistency of women.

LESTER: There's a letter from a man in Ohio. He says, I am in love with a girl who won't even go out with me. She thinks only big, strong men are romantic.

MAE: I met a guy once. The only thing strong about him was his breath!

LESTER: (shocked but very serious.) That's not this man's trouble.

MAE: Oh. (MAE steals a glance INTO CAMERA and rolls her eyes.)

LESTER: (reading) I joined an Athletic Club to develop my muscles but all I developed was a charley horse. And I lost ten pounds. Should I give up this girl because I'm a pencil-pusher and not a muscle man?

MAE: Honey, all men are muscle men. You're just pushing your pencil in the wrong direction! Write her a romantic poem or love note, and tell her how you feel. I'll be willing to bet she goes out with you and gets a big bang out of it.

LESTER makes a note on the pad, taking her remarks at face value. His lack of reaction is provocative to Mae. She rises and moves around him slowly, eyeing him like a piece of merchandise she's considering buying.

MAE   Lester, do you have a middle name?

LESTER   Yes, but I don't use it.

MAE pauses behind him, and puts her hands on her hips.

MAE   (sexy) Is it… Lamb?

LESTER understands this comment, and anticipates where she is going with it. He doesn't dare look at her.

LESTER   No.

MAE   Is it… Angel?

LESTER is very uncomfortable. He tries to put an end to the subject by becoming very matter-of-fact.

LESTER   No. And you'll never guess it. It starts with an X.

MAE is genuinely surprised.

MAE   What is it?

LESTER   I'd rather not say.

> MAE moves closer to LESTER, and touches his muscular bicep.

MAE   Come on… You can tell me…

LESTER   I'd rather not.

MAE   Don't be silly.

LESTER   I don't like the name.

> LESTER moves and sits on the foot of the chaise to get away from her. He grabs another letter and changes the subject by quickly reading. Amused, she lets him escape her this time.

LESTER   Dear Miss West, I am six foot five inches and weigh two hundred and fifty pounds. My girlfriend is four foot ten inches tall and weighs eighty-five pounds. Is a marriage between us practical?

MAE   That depends on how ingenious you are. I'd say marry the girl. Of course, you may have to shake out the bedclothes to find her.

LESTER   (picks up another letter.) This is from a man in Indiana. My girlfriend likes to get herself all gussied up with jazzy clothes. We are invited to a wedding and I said I wouldn't go unless she wore a sweater and skirt. She fooled me…

MAE   (interjects) Naturally.

LESTER   …and she found a skirt covered all over with sequins. Will you please tell her not to buy it? The

	skirt may be all right for the wedding but it's just too flashy for the things we generally do.
MAE	Let her buy it. When you're doing the things you generally do… don't let her wear the skirt.
LESTER	Oh. It's so obvious.

MAE looks INTO CAMERA and rolls her eyes.

The TELEPHONE RINGS. MAE picks up the receiver.

MAE	Yes, Josephine. (pause) Oh?

MAE holds the receiver away from her ear while she thinks.

LESTER	Anything wrong?
MAE	(unsure) Harry is here. I invited him to come up and see me sometime. And he came over for lunch.
LESTER	But you just had lunch with George.
MAE	But I hate to send Harry away. He's such a nice guy.
LESTER	Then let him eat lunch. You don't have to.
MAE	Hmmm… maybe a little dessert. (into the phone) I'll be out in a minute, Josephine.

MAE replaces the receiver. LESTER is ready with the next letter.

LESTER	From a fourteen-year old girl. Dear Miss West, are you for real?

MAE	(Laughs) You can believe it! I materialized one night, plucked an apple off a tree – handed it to some bloke – and I've been real ever since!
	LESTER smiles as he makes a note.
LESTER	(thinking aloud) I thought that tree had something to do with right and wrong.
MAE	Honey, wrong has nothing to do with it!
	Distracted, MAE picks up a hand mirror and plumps her hair.
MAE	(slyly) Does the X in your name stand for Xavier (Zav-ier)?
LESTER	(wary) No.
MAE	Oh… hmmm… Xenocrates (Zen-oc-ra-tees)?
LESTER	No.
	LESTER quickly picks up a letter and begins to read.
LESTER	Dear Mae West, I want to get married but my boyfriend is a real Casper Milquetoast. We've been going together for months, but he's so shy he's afraid to kiss me.
	MAE shoots a meaningful glance at LESTER, and then INTO CAMERA.
MAE	I know somebody like that.

LESTER   (reading the letter) I decided the next time he brings me home from the movies, I'm going to grab him and kiss him. My girlfriend says I shouldn't do it because it might scare him. Should I go on waiting for him to kiss me, or should I scare him?

Mae West at her Santa Monica beach house, 1954.

MAE   Honey, that lamb needs to be scared… stiff!

               MAE exits through the door as the THEME MUSIC plays.

               FADE OUT.

               THE END.

Once the actress expressed an interest in exploring television ideas, many comedy writers clamored to present pilot proposals to Mae and her representatives. *MAE WEST TELLS ALL ABOUT LOVE* is the only remaining alternate pilot to be found.

MAE WEST TELLS ALL ABOUT LOVE

ANNOUNCER Ladies and gentlemen… the Fabulous… MAE… WEST!

SUDDENLY EVERYTHING AROUND THE WORLD STOPS.

(STOCK SHOTS) A GROUP OF WORKMEN IN A SHIPYARD STOP DEAD IN THE THEIR TRACKS… TWO HOUSEWIVES HANGING CLOTHES ON THE LINE STOP… A CHINESE RICKSHAW RUNNER STOPS… A STEAMSHIP OUT AT SEA STOPS DEAD IN THE WATER…

SUDDENLY, UNDER THIS MONTAGE, THE ANNOUNCER'S VOICE IS HEARD.

ANNOUNCER Yes, ladies and gentlemen. We proudly present… the one and only… the FABULOUS… MAE… WEST!!

MAE WEST makes a sweeping entrance the long way around the whole studio stage set, and after circling the set that looks like her personal living room, she stops beside an ornate chaise

	longue. Resting one hand on the decorative chaise, and the other on her hip, she smiles INTO CAMERA.
MAE	Ummm… hello.
	CUT TO MAE WEST'S SECRETARY, A YOUNG BODYBUILDER WHOSE BODY IS SQUEEZED INTO TIGHT CLOTHING. HE IS SITTING ON A CHAIR BESIDE THE CHAISE. A LARGE ATHLETE'S GYM BAG IS ON THE FLOOR BY HIS FEET.
	CLOSE SHOT: SECRETARY.
SECRETARY	Ladies and gentlemen. This is a sensational event in my life as for the first time on television, the eternally glamorous Miss Mae West will answer some of the many letters you have sent in since the announcement that she would appear on this program. I must add, however, that Miss West's expressed opinions do not necessarily reflect those of this station… any other station… the United Nations… Mr. America… or Mrs. America… Iran… Iraq… or the Virgin Islands!
MAE	Hold it… hold it! You've gone far enough! Let's get down to business at your hands, and read me some of those letters.
	MAE sits back comfortably on the chaise. The format from this point consists of the SECRETARY reading letters to MAE WEST, and MAE

answering while admiring herself in a hand mirror, primping her hair, squirting perfume on herself, flicking a delicate silk scarf, or admiring her polished finger nails.

The SECRETARY opens his gym bag, reaches in and removes a jump rope.

MAE (glances into the camera) Oh…

The SECRETARY reaches into his bag again and removes dumbbells.

MAE (looking into the camera) Hmmm…

The SECRETARY reaches into his bag again and removes a pair of boxing gloves.

MAE (looking into the camera and rolling her eyes) I see…

The SECRETARY reaches into his bag and finally pulls out a stack of letters. He unfolds the first letter.

SECRETARY Dear Miss West, I am a widow in Chicago with my two tiny children. Recently, I met a very wealthy man who wants to marry me, and already just loves my children. He is always wanting to give them presents and asking me to suggest something suitable. What would you suggest? Signed, Chicago Widow.

MAE Dear Chicago Widow. Since you say your children are so tiny, and your man is so wealthy, I'd

> suggest a set of blocks. About six nice blocks… along Michigan Avenue.
>
> MAE addresses her SECRETARY.

MAE
: Mmmm… You know, honey, you're doin' just great!

SECRETARY
: (shyly) Well, thank you.

MAE
: What did you say your name is, dear?

SECRETARY
: Rex.

MAE
: Rex! That's a kingly name. (she looks him over) You may be king-sized, dear, but remember. I'm filter tipped!

> REX appears embarrassed.

MAE
: What's your full name, sexy Rexy?

REX
: Rex May.

MAE
: Mmmmm… is that so? Well, hang around… and I may too.

> REX squirms in his seat.

MAE
: Now, back to the business in your hands.

REX
: What?

MAE
: The letters, dear. The letters.

REX
: Oh. Right. (reads next letter) Dear Miss West, I am the mother of seventeen children, but my husband has been out of work, and we find it necessary to go on relief. On top of this, we now

	find that there is no record of our marriage at city hall. Is there anything we can do? Signed, Bewitched, bothered and uncomfortable.
MAE	It seems to me you've done enough. A little relief now and then may be the answer. I wouldn't say that city hall has lost your record. They're just trying to keep up with it!
REX	Dear Miss West, I am a concert violinist and have fallen in love with a strip tease artist, but most of my friends seem to disapprove. They think our fields are too far apart. Do you think we could ever find anything in common? Signed, The Fiddler.
MAE	Dear Fiddler. I know one thing you have in common… if it's only a G String.
REX	Dear Miss West, I am an ex-racketeer and I now own a big used car lot, see? I've fallen for a cute little red-head, see? She has her eye on one of my Cadillacs. I don't know if she likes me for myself or the Cadillac, see? But she always wants me to take her out in the same car. Is something wrong here? My parole officer suggested I write to you, see? Signed, Pen Pal.
MAE	There's nothing wrong with taking little red for a ride, you hood. See?
REX	Dear Miss West, my boyfriend is a photographer. Many times when I walk into the studio, I

	invariably find him with his arms around one of his models. He says he is just setting her up in a pose, and that I am the only one he really goes for. Would you accept a proposal from a man like this? Signed, In the Dark.
MAE	Hmmmm… that all depends on what he'd propose! With the proper exposure, something might develop!
REX	Dear Miss West, I love to stay home and cook and sew, and I do just lovely embroidery, but my wife is always complaining. She just insists that I write you for some little helpful suggestion. Signed, Undecided.
MAE	Well, let me answer that this way. Dear Mrs. Undecided, why not turn the table and get yourself a job as a welder. Or maybe a truck driver. You know… a little tit for tat!
	REX appears taken aback.
MAE	(looks into the camera) Well… I ain't Dear Abby!
REX	Dear Miss West, my boyfriend is always comparing me to you! And since I don't have all of your special endowments, I still think I have plenty to offer. Yet, he continues to idolize you, and holds you so high on a pedestal, that I'm ready to give up! What do you suggest? Signed, Miss East.

MAE   Dear Miss East! Give up! After all, let's face it. East is east… and West… is West!

REX   Dear Miss West, my husband Joe is short and stout, and holds a very important executive position with his firm, yet every time I arrive at his office unexpectedly, I find he is also holding his secretary on his lap. My complaints seem to fall on deaf ears, as he assures me that this is only for effect and strictly a part of office procedure. I love little Joe, but do you think I'm getting a fair shake? Signed, Standing Room Only.

MAE   Well, I'm not one to break up a home, but in this case, I'd leave little Joe… holding the bag!

REX   Do you need a break, Miss West?

MAE   Don't stop now, honey, we're on a roll.

REX   Dear Miss West, I know that this sounds silly for a grown school teacher, but I am afraid I am letting romantic notions bother me lately. I am very fond of Mr. X, one of my colleagues, who seems to like me very much. Yet, I must admit I also have eyes for the principal of the school. I know that the principal is financially secure, but Mr. X also has a fine position. What would you do? Signed, Shop-worn School Teacher.

MAE   Well, of course, position is everything in life… but I'd find out… how much interest I could

	draw from the principle!
REX	Dear Miss West, we are trapeze artists, and spend most of our time working out on a trapeze. Consequently, our love life suffers. There must be some remedy for this. Can you help? Signed, Up in the Air.
MAE	Ummm... well, I must admit. I've never had a work-out on a swing. It seems to me it would only be a question of... balance!
REX	Dear Miss West, we have been house hunting. My husband prefers a small home with one bath, while I prefer the larger type home with two baths. This is causing us a great deal of argument. Would you want to suggest some solution? Signed, Restless.
MAE	Well, dear. Sounds to me like your husband has been watching too many soap operas. He's just putting up a defense against – his wife's other John!
REX	Dear Miss West, my husband spends all of his spare time every weekend mowing our front lawn, but he never discards the grass! He just piles it up until it's beginning to look like a load of hay! All of our neighbors are complaining, but he just laughs it off....
MAE	He does what?!

REX   Laughs it off.

MAE   Oh, excuse me. Go on.

REX   …but he just laughs it off. Do you think he could have any ulterior motive? Or am I worrying needlessly? Signed, Grass Widow.

MAE   Well, dear, it's time to worry when you find him lost in the hay!

REX   Dear Miss West, I am a married woman with a little money. I've already spent over one hundred thousand dollars on my current husband. He dabbles in theatricals, and so far we have three children, with another on the way, but this expense is killing me. What do I do now? Signed, Over-Burdened.

MAE   Dear over-load… I mean over-burdened. Shell out, dear, and be grateful! It's a little late for a refund!

REX   Dear Miss West, recently my boyfriend asked me to marry him. He is a plumber and makes a terrific salary, still we are never invited anywhere. I am beginning to feel like a social outcast. I'm afraid our marriage will go down the drain. Do you think I should marry a plumber? Signed, All Choked Up.

MAE   There's certainly nothing wrong with a plumber. Of course, it's better if he has the right pipes, nuts and U-joints!

REX   Dear Miss West, I recently became engaged to

	John, a very handsome fellow, but since taking an ocean trip I've met another very charming man named Dick. In all fairness, I can't make up my mind what to do about John. Do you think I should leave the door open? Signed, A Loose End.
MAE	Well, an open door can lead to a closed corporation! In fact, I've always believed in an open door policy!
REX	Dear Miss West, my boyfriend is a born beachcomber and just adores surf-board riding. He even seems to prefer his surf-board to me. Don't you think this is wrong? Signed, High and Dry.
MAE	Dear High and Dry. Very frankly, I can't see anything wrong in riding a wave!
REX	Dear Miss West, my husband is a teacher of English, yet so many times when we are alone, conversation between us is most frustrating. He doesn't seem to even finish his sentences. One thought so quickly leads to another, that by the time he has finished yakking, I am left high and dry for an explanation. This is getting me nowhere. How do you explain it? Signed, Frustrated Wife.
MAE	Hmm… well, English or no English, this guy is obviously dangling his… participles!
REX	Dear Miss West, my apartment house manager

	claims to be so much in love with me, yet he never fixes up little things around the apartment, and even wants to raise my rent again. I can hardly stand another raise. What would you do? Signed, Just Floored.
MAE	(smiles slyly and turns INTO CAMERA.) Hmmm... it must be time for one of those commercials.

CAMERA PULLS OUT revealing MAE and REX on the glamorous set.

ANNOUNCER V.O. To all our friends out there, Miss West will welcome any and all letters you may care to write should you have a problem you would like to discuss – especially affairs of the heart. You may sign your letters with any identifying signature you may wish to use, and send them to Miss West in care of this station. All letters thus received will remain confidential, and those she is able to answer, will be answered exactly as you would expect them to be answered... by a true expert!

FADE OUT

THE END.

The Mae West Show was also proposed as a radio series. Several treatments and scripts were offered for the actress's consideration. The premise of Mae answering letters was similar, but the radio program was designed to include special guest stars for each episode.

With the rising popularity of television, however, radio programs were quickly becoming obsolete. Nothing came of the idea.

The only remaining radio pilot is also titled, *The Mae West Show*. The cast included an Announcer, Mae's maid Ruby, and proposed special guest Gene Autry.

ANNOUNCER And now it's my pleasure to introduce the most fabulous woman in the world… you've seen her on the stage in *Diamond Lil*… you've thrilled to her in the movies… and now (Name of Product) brings you the only woman of whom men, both young and old have been known to remark (WOLF WHISTLE) – the one and only MAE WEST!

RUBY Just a moment, Mr. Hannibal. But before we introduce Miss West, I've got to make sure. Is the temperature seventy-two and a half degrees?

ANNOUNCER Yes.

RUBY Are the pillows all fluffed up?

ANNOUNCER But of course.

RUBY Has her favorite incense been lighted?

ANNOUNCER Naturally.

RUBY Alright, then…

SOUND: KNOCK… KNOCK.

RUBY (Cont.) Miss West, everything has been attended to… Can I do anything else?

MAE Yes, Ruby, peel me a grape.

SOUND: DOOR OPENING.

ANNOUNCER Best of luck on your opening show, Miss West!

MAE Thank you, Hannibal. It was nice of you to come up and see me... and while I'm on the subject, I want to extend an invitation to all of you to come up and see me at this time.

ANNOUNCER Well, what kind of show is this going to be?

MAE It's gonna be a brand new type of show for men, with some very interesting men and from time to time we're gonna talk about some very fascinating subjects, which are very interesting to men.

ANNOUNCER Why, Miss West, don't you think of anything else besides men?

MAE If I do, I'm not thinking!

ANNOUNCER You like men, I gather?

MAE I like the men *I* gather.

ANNOUNCER Well, to get back to the show. What is it going to be about?

MAE We'll have some fun and laughs... I'm gonna give a little advice to the love-worn... I mean lovelorn... tell a bedtime story... and once in a while I may touch on a few hot news items. And incidentally listeners, I want you to write and tell me what you want... and if it's too exciting... telegraph!

ANNOUNCER	Is the program just going to be for young, single men?
MAE	No, it will include married men, too.
ANNOUNCER	Married men, too?
MAE	You know what a married man is… that's a bachelor with the nerve removed… but I'm talking too much. Before I exert myself any more… Ruby?
RUBY	Yes, Miss West.
MAE	Will you play some music? I'm in the mood to be soothed.
	MUSIC "I WANNA BE LOVED" PLAYS
MAE	(Cont.) With music like that, life can be beautiful. Alright, Hannibal, what's next?
ANNOUNCER	We have hundreds of letters here, Miss West, all seeking advice from your fabulous fountain of experience.
MAE	Well, read one to me.
ANNOUNCER	This is from a listener in Chicago. She writes: Dear Miss West. Recently I met a tall, dark and handsome man, with a charming personality. He has been extremely attentive to me, and I feel myself attracted to him. However, I've just found out he's worth twelve million dollars. My friends say you can never be happy with a man who is spoiled with that much money. Signed, J.C.

MAE   Dear J.C. Your friends are absolutely right. This man is not for you. You can be much happier with a sincere, hard-working man, who may not make a lot of money, but at least you'll know he'll be there every night. Incidentally, what is the name of the man with the twelve million dollars? What's next, Hannibal?

ANNOUNCER   This is from R.W. She says: Dear Miss West. I am 26 years old, and have a very strict guardian. First, I was going out with a boy who smoked cigarettes, and she objected to him. Then I went with a boy who drank, and she disapproved of him, too. Recently, I have been going out with a boy who only likes to hug me and kiss me at every opportunity, and yet she approves of him. What shall I do? Signed, Anxious.

MAE   Dear Anxious. Pay attention to your guardian. She is only trying to show you that you can have just as much fun in life without smoking and drinking. And now, Hannibal.

ANNOUNCER   Here is one from a worried mother. She says: Dear Miss West. I have a young son who has now reached the age where he is starting to ask embarrassing questions. Shall I tell him about the birds and the bees? Signed, C.R.

MAE   Dear C.R. I would go easy on the birds and the bees. I once knew a kid who was told so much

	about the birds and bees that when he reached 18 years of age, he fell in love with sparrow…
ANNOUNCER	Here's another, Miss West. She says: Dear Miss West. I have been going steady with a man for the past 25 years, and so far, he has not popped the question. Under these circumstances, do you think I can look forward to any kind of security?
MAE	Yes, dearie. Social Security! Hannibal, are there any other letters?
ANNOUNCER	Yes, here's a hot one from your lawyer.
MAE	Well, put it in the deep freeze, and let's have a little music.
	MUSIC PLAYS. POPULAR SONG OF THE DAY.
ANNOUNCER	And now, Miss West, we have a guest for you. It's none other than that fabulous cowboy star of stage, screen and television… GENE AUTRY!
MAE	Hi'ya, Gene! Why don't cha come up and lasso me sometime?
GENE	Awful nice to meet you, Ma'am.
MAE	Say, Gene, how are things in the wild and woolly West?
GENE	You know, Mae, the best part of the West is in *Diamond Lil*.

MAE	You know there's a lot more to these cowboys than you see on television.
GENE	I saw you in *Diamond Lil*, Mae, and I think you're wonderful, you're marvelous, you're terrific.
MAE	Easy, Gene… you're being unfair to your horse.
GENE	Now, Mae, in our part of the country, a horse has its place and a woman has her place, too.
MAE	Well, that sounds like a good arrangement to me. Don't you ever meet any cowgirls out there?
GENE	Cowgirls?
MAE	Surely you know what a cowgirl is?
GENE	Shucks, Mae, all cows are girls.
MAE	You're just a boy, aren't you?
GENE	You know, Mae, I'd like to take you out to Texas.
MAE	I don't know if it's big enough for me.
GENE	Big enough? Why in Texas you can get on a train one day, ride three days and at the end of the third day, you're still in Texas!
MAE	We've got those same kind of trains in New York City.
GENE	We've got awful brave men in Texas. Did you ever hear of Davy Crockett, Sam Houston? Do you have brave men like that in New York?

MAE	I guess you've never umpired a game at Ebbets Field.
GENE	You've never lived until you've been at a rodeo in Dallas. You should see the rip-roaring, snortin' broncs in Texas.
MAE	You should see the rip-roaring, snortin' Bronx in New York!
GENE	In Texas, when a man gets married he buys his wife a horse and makes her learn to ride that horse.
MAE	In New York, when a man gets married he buys his wife a house and makes her learn to work like a horse!
GENE	Gee, Mae, I sure would like to put my brand on you.
MAE	The only brands I'm interested in come from Tiffany's.
GENE	Mae, that's a big honor. Why, in Texas, a horse is proud to wear its owner's brand.
MAE	Well, Gene, women are a little different than horses… they require more carats. MUSIC UP: "DIAMONDS ARE A GIRL'S BEST FRIEND."
ANNOUNCER	Now comes time for one of our most enjoyable features of this program, your bedtime story…

	for men only. What have you chosen for your story tonight, Miss West?
MAE	It is the story of the Fairy Princess and the Little Frog.
ANNOUNCER	Can we hear it?
MAE	Yes, I have it right here. Ruby, will you read it?
RUBY	Once upon a time, in a Kingdom far away, there lived a little princess.
MAE	Those storytellers are no dopes, they always start out, "Once upon a time," and it always takes place in a mythical Kingdom, so that if you wanted to check up on the girl's age, where are you going to find her birth certificate? Go on, Ruby…
RUBY	One day, this little princess went into the royal garden, and was playing with her golden ball…
MAE	Everybody was so rich in those days, they even had diamond yo-yos for wealthy idiots.
RUBY	While the princess was playing she suddenly came upon a frog.
MAE	A wandering Frenchman, no doubt.
RUBY	Just as she was about to step on the frog, the frog yelled, "Don't step on me, little princess!"
MAE	How those kids could always tell what the animals are saying is beyond me. I have trouble

	understanding my tax collector, and he is really a beast. Go on, Ruby.
RUBY	The little princess stooped down and picked up the little frog in her hand.
MAE	I heard they give you warts.
RUBY	As it grew towards evening, the little frog said, "Princess, will you take me home with you tonight, because I am really not a frog, but just enchanted. Do you believe me?" And the princess said, "Certainly, because I am enchanted, too."
MAE	Some enchanted evening…
RUBY	So, the little princess took the little frog into the castle, and put him under warm blankets in her playroom.
MAE	He would have been better off on a hot plate, with a little tartar sauce.
RUBY	Then the princess went into her own room and fell fast asleep. When she awoke in the morning, she went into the playroom, and what do you suppose happened to the frog?
MAE	Don't tell me he turned into Hopalong Cassidy!
RUBY	No. Standing there in his place was a tall, handsome prince, and he asked the princess to marry him, and she did, and they lived happily ever after.
MAE	Is that all?

RUBY	Yes, Miss West. Why?
MAE	I'm just wondering whether her mother believed *that* story!
	MUSIC. POPULAR SONG OF THE DAY.
ANNOUNCER	And now, before we say goodnight, Miss West, may we have your moral for today?
MAE	Naturally. Here's a little advice to you men. When you're courtin' women, remember this. Candy is dandy, but a jewel makes 'em drool. Goodnight, kiddies!

THE END

CHAPTER 6

Mae West Meets Dean Martin and Bob Hope

"You watch your television programs. I'll watch mine!"

WHEN MAE FINISHED THE draft of her autobiography, she resumed her nightclub tour in 1959. She performed in the Starlite Room at the Chi-Chi in Palm Springs from March 15 through March 22, and at the Sahara Hotel in Las Vegas from March 24 until April 13.

Mae then returned to Los Angeles and began rehearsing for her first guest-starring role in a television variety show. She was paid $15,000 to perform on *The Dean Martin (Variety) Show* (1959-1960) which was taped in Studio 1 at NBC in Burbank. Rehearsals lasted several days. The show, also starring Bob Hope, was recorded on tape on Thursday, April 30. Filmed in color, the program aired on Sunday night, May 3, 1959. Network executives closely watched program content, especially for variety shows. Mae did not write her lines, and was forced to work with a script approved by network bosses and censors. Nevertheless, she stole the show with her insinuations, asides, and perfect timing. Dean worked hard to keep up with her.

"He was a handsome guy," Mae told biographer Charlotte Chandler, "and he had a good line, speaking of sex personalities. He said to me, 'Call me Dino.'"

Martin's image, one that he encouraged, gave the impression that was drinking on the air to the point of being inebriated. "People said he performed drunk," the actress recalled. "I don't think so. I never saw him drunk. He was naturally a high guy, so he didn't need anything, though I'm sure he knew how to drink if he wanted to. I found him very professional, and he cared too much about the show to do anything to jeopardize it. Playing like he'd been drinking was part of his public personality for his act. He made everybody feel good because he shared his good mood with the other performers and with the audience. He saved any bad mood he ever had for in private. He was a professional, and he had an image to safeguard. I know what's that like."

Mae makes her entrance.

Timex sponsored Martin's show. The advertising tagline read, "For an evening of music, fun and culture, may we recommend this once-in-a-lifetime trio: Dean, Mae, and Bob!" Her upcoming appearance was promoted weeks in advance.

The program opened with Dean and Bob joking and singing. Mae made her entrance about twenty minutes into the one-hour show.

SCENE ONE.

SOUND: DOORBELL RINGS

DOOR OPENS, IN WALKS A HERALD CARRYING A TRUMPET. HE PLAYS OPENING OF THE SONG "FRANKIE AND JOHNNY."

MUSIC: ORCHESTRA PLAYS PETER GUNN-TYPE MUSIC. TWO MORE MEN ENTER AND STAND ON EITHER SIDE OF THE DOOR.

Mae West.

MUSIC: GROWS LOUDER. IN WALKS MAE WEST DRESSED TO THE HILT. MAE ENTERS, SWAYS AROUND THE ROOM GIVING IT THE ONCE-OVER. A MAN COMES OVER, TAKES OFF HER FEATHERED BOA.

Mae and her personal Cub Scout.

MAE　　　Take it easy. That ostrich is still alive.

MAE SAUNTERS OVER TO DEAN AND SIZES HIM UP.

MAE	Good evening, Ed.
DEAN	Ed?

Mae meets Dean Martin.

MAE	Sure. You know with me everything is *Person to Person*.
MAE	(Cont. to the MEN) All right, boys, I'll call you if I need you. Stand right outside the door.
DEAN	Oh, you don't have to worry.
MAE	And don't let anybody in.

DEAN	What are they? Are they your bodyguards?
MAE	No. It's the Cub Scout patrol. They're working on their merit badge.
DEAN	Mae, make yourself comfortable, and sit right here, dear.
MAE	Well… well…
DEAN	Sit down because we may not be back this way. Now that we're here in my studio, how do you like TV so far?
MAE	I haven't made up my mind yet. I'm waiting for the Late, Late Show.
DEAN	I see you're familiar with TV.
MAE	Oh, I watch it all the time.
DEAN	What's your favorite program?
MAE	Those Vic Tanny commercials!
DEAN	What time are they on?
MAE	I wouldn't know. I don't have a set.
DEAN	But you just said…
MAE	You watch your television programs. I'll watch mine!
DEAN	Well, anyway Mae, I want to tell you what a pleasure it is having you as my guest tonight.
MAE	The pleasure is all mine, tall, dark, and Neapolitan.

DEAN	I must say, you're as beautiful as ever.
MAE	You're not so bad yourself. Say, would you mind getting me a cushion?
DEAN	(obliges) You know, I'm really looking forward to our duet.
MAE	Yeah? What have you got in mind?
DEAN	"I Can't Give You Anything But Love!"
MAE	You had me worried. I thought we were going to sing.
DEAN	We are! That's the name of the song!
MAE	Oh, you crooners are all alike. You get alone with a girl and all you want to do is sing to her. Don't you want a little bon voyage kiss?
DEAN	Bon voyage? I'm not sailing.
MAE	Wanna bet? (she holds his face and gives him a kiss)
DEAN	All ashore who's going ashore!
MAE	And you wanted to sing.
DEAN	Oh, yeah… our duet. Now look, Mae. See, television isn't like the movies. You don't have to memorize anything. We've got all the lyrics written down on cue cards.
MAE	Cue cards?
DEAN	That fellow over there – he's holding them. If you forget a line, just look at the cards.

Mae and Dino.

MAE   All right. All right. Stop nagging. (to herself) I wonder how you get a guest shot on a Vic Tanny commercial.

DEAN   Are you ready?

MAE   Always.

DEAN   We'll sing that later.

           MUSIC: "I CAN'T GIVE YOU ANYTHING BUT LOVE, BABY"

DEAN   (singing) "I can't give you anything but love…"

MAE   I'll take it.

DEAN   "…baby… that's the only thing I've plenty of…"

MAE   I said I'll take it.

DEAN	"…baby… dream awhile scheme awhile you're sure to find…"
MAE	Go on.
DEAN	"…happiness and I guess…"
MAE	(peering at the cue card man off camera) Say, bring those cards a little closer.
DEAN	"…gee, I'd love to see you looking swell…"
MAE	(still peering off) A little closer.
DEAN	"…baby… diamond bracelets Woolworth doesn't sell…"
MAE:	(calling out to the cue card man) You've got 'em upside down!
DEAN	"…baby… till that lucky day you known darn well, baby, I can't give you anything but love."
	MUSIC: CONTINUES
DEAN	It's your turn, Mae.
MAE	Be right with you. (Calling out to the cue card man) Come here a minute.
DEAN	Mae, it's your chorus.
MAE	Don't rush me. (The cue card man comes into scene… and he's good looking) What's your name?
CUE CARD MAN	Stanley.

Mae and Stanley the Steamer.

MAE   Yeah? (Looks him over) I'll bet you're a steamer!

DEAN   (cries out) Mae!

MUSIC: INTO CHORUS

MAE   (singing and looking at STANLEY) "I can't give you anything but love, baby. That's the only thing I've plenty of. You sing a while…"

DEAN   (singing) "…dream a while, scheme a while, you're sure to find…"

MAE   (to STANLEY) You know you're kinda cute?

DEAN   (singing) "Happiness, and I guess…"

MAE   (to STANLEY) What are you doing after the show?

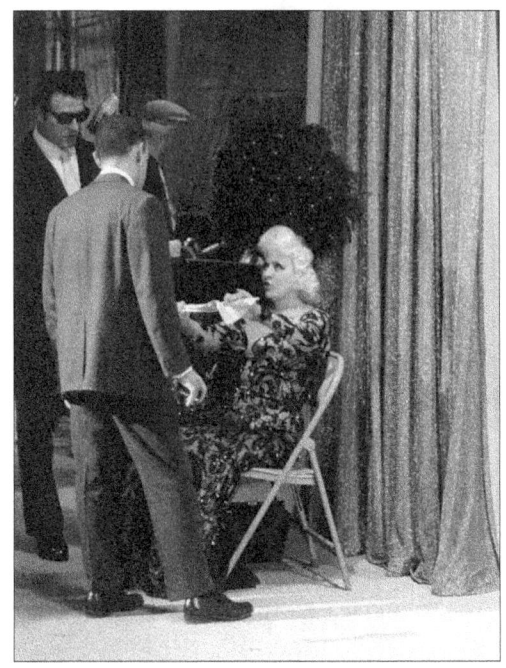

Mae rests offstage with Paul Novak, wearing sunglasses, watching over her.

STANLEY   Oh, probably going bowling with the fellas. Have a few beers.

DEAN   (singing) "…gee, I'd like to see you looking swell, baby…"

MAE   (to STANLEY) How about coming up to my place?

STANLEY   (as DEAN continues to sing) Can we have a few beers?

MAE   Yeah, after we go bowling!

STANLEY   (throws down cue cards dramatically, and sings)

	"Till that lucky day you know darn well…"
MAE	(handing cue cards to DEAN) Here – hold the cards.
STANLEY	(singing) "…baby, I can't give you anything…"
MAE	Sing it! (to DEAN) Hold the cards up so Stanley can see them!
STANLEY	(singing) "I can't give you anything but love!"

MAE WEST RECLINES.

END SCENE ONE

SCENE TWO

DEAN and BOB play an extended scene in tuxedos singing and playing golf, surrounded by beautiful female caddies. They sing a duet of "Put It There, Pal."

DEAN	That's the song you sang with Bing in *Road to Utopia*.
BOB	There was another great song in that picture…
MAE'S V.O.	Pardon me… may I play through? (DEAN and BOB look up as MAE enters the scene in a personalized golf cart, dressed in a glittering gown. She's carrying a glittering rhinestone putter. MAE climbs out of the golf cart, and straightens her dress.) Sorry to intrude, but I just got out of a trap.

Mae enters in her personalized golf cart.

BOB		Bunker?

MAE		I don't know what his name was! But anyway, I happened to hear you talking about a song from *Road to Utopia*.

DEAN		You know the one we mean?

MAE		Know it? It's the story of my life!

		MUSIC: for the song "Personality."

MAE		(singing) "When Madame Pompadour was on the ballroom floor, said all the gentlemen, obviously, the Madame has the cutest, personality."

DEAN		(singing) "And think of all the books, about DuBarry's looks…"

BOB	(singing) "…what was it made her the toast of Paree?"
MAE	(singing) "…the lady has a perfect personality…"
DEAN	(singing) "…and why are certain girls, offered certain things…"
BOB	(singing) "…like sable coats, and wedding rings by men who wear their hats right…"
ALL	"That's right!"
MAE	(singing) "Men open charge accounts, for me in large amounts, at Cartier and Tiffany, because they seem to like my, personality…"
ALL	(singing) "Per-son-al-i-ty!"
MAE	Thank you boys. Oh, Stanley!

STANLEY appears in a tuxedo, carrying her golf bag and clubs.

MAE	Tee me!

STANLEY takes out a golf ball covered in glittering rhinestone. MAE attaches it to her glittering charm bracelet.

MAE	See you 'round, boys! (to STANLEY) Oh, Stanley?
STANLEY	Yes.
MAE	Peel me a grape! (MAE saunters off, followed by STANLEY)

END SCENE TWO

Mae and Dean and Bob.

Mae West sang "Diamonds Are a Girl's Best Friend," surrounded by Dean and Bob and a group of beautiful young women.

Mae and Dean and Bob.

FINAL SCENE AT SHOW END

DEAN   Mae, honey, what can I say? You can come up and see me any time at all.

MAE   Thank you, Dean. I loved being here, and you know, you're alright. You've got quite a style, you know. As a matter of fact, I'm calling up Vic Tanny and I'm telling him if he's smart, he'll go to you.

THE END.

Mae sings, "Diamonds Are a Girl's Best Friend."

Goodness Had Nothing To Do With It.

CHAPTER 7

Person to Person. On again, off again

"Nowadays, you don't hide your past. You print it."

IT WAS SELF-PROMOTION RATHER than an acting role that lured Mae West back to television. In late summer, 1959, Prentice Hall published her long-awaited autobiography *Goodness Had Nothing To Do With It*. Reviews were mixed, but sales quickly made the book a bestseller. Her friend, Hunt Stromberg Jr. invited her to be interviewed by Charles Collingwood on the 7th season premiere of the popular interview program, *Person to Person*. Collingwood replaced the show's creator, Edward R. Morrow, who had hosted the first six seasons. Stromberg, whose father was a respected producer at MGM, was gay and well-connected. He had recently become the head of West Coast programming for CBS-TV.

Mae thought it would be a wonderful opportunity to promote her book. Originally, she wanted the interview to take place in her Santa Monica beach house. She wasn't keen on hosting a film crew in her more private – and much smaller – apartment. Publicity photographs for the scheduled interview were taken at the beach house, but ultimately, it was decided the apartment would be a better location.

Mae with Charles Collingwood at her Santa Monica beach house.

On October 4, Charles Collingwood and a film crew arrived at the Ravenswood to tape the program. It was a long day in front of the camera, but the interview was completed. Hours of video tape would ultimately be edited down to approximately twelve minutes of air time. CBS enthusiastically promoted her rare TV appearance on the season premiere of *Person to Person*, scheduled to be broadcast at 10:30 pm, PST, on October 16.

However, Los Angeles and New York newspapers surprised the public, and Mae herself, when their morning headlines announced that her scheduled appearance on the show that evening had been cancelled! The *Los Angeles Times* heralded, "Suggestive at 64! Mae

West Censored From New TV Show!" and "CBS-TV Cancels Mae West Show: Fears a Taped Interview on *Person to Person* Program Might Be Misconstrued!" The *Los Angeles Herald Express* wrote, "TV Says Mae West Too Hot to Handle!"

Network executives watched the taped interview the day before, and got cold feet. They announced the cancellation tersely, "In the opinion of the network, it was felt that certain portions of the interview with Mae West might be misconstrued."

Mae was in San Francisco on a legal matter when she was notified. "I don't know what they could have misconstrued," she mused. "Certain minds always misconstrue everything. I have a very big public that understands what I say. I was asked questions from my autobiography, which is honest and frank and deals with sex all the way through the book. In my apartment I have a nude statue of myself and maybe they objected to that. The program showed my bedroom and bed and I was standing by it. But I did wear a very sedate, dignified gown. I only went on the show for my book."

John A. Aaron and Jesse Zousmer, who produced *Person to Person* for CBS, said, "The show speaks for itself, and so does Miss West." Val Adams, a reporter for the *Los Angeles Times*, viewed the interview at a press screening, and described the show as a "typical Mae West performance." Cecil Smith, *Los Angeles Times* Entertainment Editor, agreed. He wrote, "I looked at the offending tape last night and found little in it that might offend anyone – even a confirmed bluenose. It was scheduled to be shown at 10:30 tonight, when the kiddies are presumably in bed. The rolling West gait was there – rolling as nimbly as it has been for 45 years on stage and screen. The throaty voice was there and as suggestive as ever. But it would not have been Mae West without them. The dialogue was typically Westian."

Mae at the piano in her Ravenswood apartment.

In the controversial show, the interview began with the actress seated in her living room. She playfully answered questions. Then, Charles Collingwood followed Mae as she slinked into her famed bedroom. The oft-photographed room was decorated in white and gold, and large mirrors were mounted on the wall behind, and above, her bed. "Why so many mirrors?" he asked.

She replied, "For personal observation. I like to know what I look like when I'm sleeping."

The reporter steered the conversation to her newly released book. "It's about my private transgressions – that's a long word for sin," she explained. "Nowadays you don't hide your past. You print it."

"Do you have much interest in foreign affairs?" he asked.

"I always had a weakness for foreign affairs," she purred. "Check chapters five and nine in my book."

Collingwood asked, "Have you had a rash of visitors since making your famous invitation, 'come up and see me sometime'?"

"I'll say! I had to install two steel doors. Now I suppose someone will come up with a blowtorch!"

"Have you ever given advice to the lovelorn?" he asked.

"Lots of times, especially my telephone number!"

The reporter asked, "What do you like reading?"

"Oh… biographies, metaphysics and psychology."

"Straight fiction?"

"Never," she said. "I can dream up my own."

"Man in space?" Collingwood wondered.

"That's a waste. Of man, I mean."

"Any advice for teenagers?"

"Yes. Grow up."

"Do you have reflections on life?" he asked.

"Yes," she said, smiling. "I'd rather have life in my men than a man in my life. Hmmmm… and a man in the house is better than two on the street. There are no withholding taxes on the wages of sin…"

Collingwood concluded with, "How does it feel to be an American institution?"

"Great! And I have the constitution to prove it!"

"Thank you for this demonstration in progressive education, and goodnight, Miss West."

"Goodnight," Mae said. "And I do like you, Charles."

The Mae West interview (scheduled to accompany an interview with her longtime friend, costume designer Edith Head) was replaced by a visit with actor James Mason and his wife, Pamela. Mae told Bob Hull of the *Los Angeles Herald Express*, "Maybe I was too good. I was very honest. And I was dressed modestly – in a full length black gown. Not low cut."

The actress was more amused by the cancellation than hurt.

Years later, she told journalist Charlotte Chandler, "When I was asked, do you have any advice for teenagers, I said, 'Grow up.' I think with that one, it wasn't so much what I said, but how I said it. I was a little on the sultry side, if you know what I mean. I could have said it a little less sultry, but that was the way it came out.

"It was all pretty innocent, I thought, but they pulled the plug on me. I was really disappointed. Then, I gave it a good think, and I wasn't so disappointed. I think I got more publicity for being canceled than I would've had if the show had gone on. So it wasn't just a waste of time, it was a waste of entertainment. I put a lot of heart into it. Maybe someday it'll turn up, and people will be more broadminded, and I'll be the broad on their minds."

Unfazed, Mae met the press in San Francisco after the cancellation of her *Person to Person* appearance.

CHAPTER 8

Mae Meets Cauliflower McPugg, San Fernando Red, and Clem Kadiddlehopper

"Well, a smart girl never beats off any man."

IN THE FOLLOWING MONTHS, *Goodness Had Nothing To Do With It*, topped the bestseller lists. Hunt Stromberg Jr. was surprised and disappointed by the way CBS handled her *Person to Person* appearance – which he helped arrange. He tried to make up for the embarrassment by offering her another shot to promote her book – and on one of CBS television's biggest hit programs – *The Red Skelton Show*.

Mae told biographer Charlotte Chandler that the network asked her to submit a script for her appearance. "I went overboard," she explained, "so they could use up their energy censoring it. Then, when they were all worn down, I submitted the script I really wanted." With the exception of a few classic West lines, the finished script was nothing less than a collaborative effort.

Skelton always employed a large staff of comedy writers including Dave O'Brien, Sherwood Schwartz, Mort Greene, Jesse Goldstein, Martin Ragaway, and Al Schwartz, among many others. Skelton contributed material as well.

Mae West visits CBS Television City in Hollywood.

The Red Skelton Show premiered on CBS in 1951. The comedy/variety show was an audience favorite for many years. The program featured comic actor Red Skelton, playing numerous recurring characters, and special guest stars. Mae West was paid $7,500 to guest star in an episode tailored for her, titled "Goodness Had Nothing To Do With It." The premise of the show was a parody of her scuttled appearance on *Person to Person*, a few months before.

William Schallert played the role of Charles Copeland, the interviewer, and Red played the roles of three men who did not appear in West's book; Cauliflower McPugg, San Fernando Red, and Clem Kadiddlehopper. Mr. Universe 1957, Reg Lewis (who was one of Mae's musclemen in her nightclub act) played the role of the muscleman. The program was recorded in black and white before a live audience in Studio 33 at CBS Television City in Los Angeles, and aired on Tuesday night, March 1, 1960.

William Shallert recalled working with Mae in a 2012 interview for the Archive of American Television. "I worked with Mae West, which was a treat and a half. She played herself. She was promoting her book. I had a few funny lines. She came on the set with this big eastern European guy with big shoulders and a bad suit. He carried her purse. He was always there to take care of all the small things for her. I got called to her dressing room so we could run lines. She was right on top of everything. But I couldn't focus on her face because she had these long eyelashes. I couldn't see through the lashes! While we were sitting there, someone opened the dressing room door. She said, 'Is anyone smoking out there!? Close the door!' I guess she thought it would affect her makeup. I don't know. She was so professional. We did our scenes together. As soon as I finished a line – bang, she was on it! I thought – the old war horse, she's really with it. She was fun to work with."

But working with Skelton was another matter for the actress. He was the kind of leading man she loathed. He preferred not to rehearse, and was skilled at ad-libbing. "His writers were so good," Shallert said, "and they were nominated for awards, but I don't know why because Red rarely did the script as written. He loved to break other people up. He loved the chaos."

Mae could hold her own with an actor who ad-libbed, as she did so well with W.C. Fields in *My Little Chickadee*, but she was not comfortable working off-book. "Mae had a few costume changes," Shallert recalled. "It only took a few minutes before she came back." In the meantime, Red took control of the stage and told jokes and stories to the audience and crew. When Mae returned, she stayed on the sidelines, and leaned against a slant board to rest without wrinkling the costume, while Red entertained the studio audience. Shallert said the director had a hard time getting him back on track and repeatedly said, "Red, Mae is ready. She's waiting."

On February 27, 1960, Mae was interviewed by Seymour Korman for the *Chicago Daily Tribune*. Korman wrote, "Mae West, apparently an indestructible sex symbol after playing that role for a generation or more, will have Red Skelton as her foil for the first time on his show."

Mae with the many persons of Red Skelton.

Mae said, "Red is unique because he has not been one of the men in my life. I've been around a long while, but the men are still fighting over me. I've got to put double locks on my doors to keep them out – I don't want more than a few around me at a time."

The reporter asked her about her bestselling book. "I wrote 600 pages and they made me cut it to 271," she explained. "That meant leaving out an awful lot of men. The guys who were left out were plenty sore about it."

The actress was asked about her feelings after CBS pulled her *Person to Person* interview. "I don't know why," she said. "I just was myself in it. What did they expect – a girl scout? We're going to use some of the stuff from that show on the Skelton program. As far as I'm concerned, the whole thing could have been shown at a church social, but I guess some of the censors have weak hearts."

OPEN:	Close up on CHARLES COPELAND. As he speaks the camera pulls out to reveal Mae West sitting on an elaborate couch in her living room. A copy of her autobiography is in her hands.
COPELAND	Good evening. This is Charles Copeland, your host on "Meet the Author." Each week at this time we interview the author of a popular book. Tonight, we're happy indeed to visit the home of the famous author of the nation's current best seller. A woman who is an American institution. Miss Mae West. Good evening, Miss West.
MAE	Good evening, Mr. Copeland.
COPELAND	First, I want to thank you for allowing us to visit you. You've been most cooperative.

MAE	That's been the secret of my success. Cooperation.
COPELAND	Now about your book Miss West. It's an autobiography.
MAE	Yes. And it's called "Goodness Had Nothin' To Do With It."
COPELAND	Isn't that title a little spicy for a life story?
MAE	Well, maybe for yours, but not for mine.
COPELAND	I see. Now, in your own words, Miss West, how would you describe your best seller?
MAE	I'd say it's a sort of sequel to the story about the birds and bees. I believe in progressive education.
COPELAND	By the way, before we go any further, please tell me this. May I feel free to ask you any questions at all?
MAE	Of course. But please use a little discretion. I understand the censor has a weak heart.
COPELAND	I'll be careful. Now, if we may, let's discuss the men in your life.
MAE	Mr. Copeland, as I've often said, it's not the men in your life that count, it's the life in your men.
COPELAND	That's true. But about those men in your life, Miss West. Have you included all of them in your book?
MAE	Oh, please! The book is only 271 pages!

COPELAND	I understand the original manuscript was over 600 pages. Did the editors boil it down?
MAE	Sort of. Well, let's say it boiled itself down.
COPELAND	I've heard. And now, how about a real exclusive for our television audience? Could we hear about the men who don't appear in your book?
MAE	You mean the men that was taken out of the book?
COPELAND	Yes.
MAE	Oh. Stand by. We're about to start a telethon!
COPELAND	Oh, Miss West, I simply meant we'd like to hear about some of the unusual men. The men who were off beat.
MAE	Well, a smart girl never beats off any man.
COPELAND	I'm talking about the extraordinary types. The characters.
MAE	Oh. Like the time I was looking for a Mr. America type for my act. I needed a man with muscles… someone strong, handsome and romantic…
	The scene fades out and fades in to a gymnasium set. CAULIFLOWER MCPUGG (Skelton) is pushing a broom around and jokes with a handsome MUSCLEMAN (Reg Lewis) who is casually working out with weights. The music swells as MAE enters.

Bodybuilder Reg Lewis.

CAULIFLOWER   Well... howdy do?

MAE   How do I do what?

Mae looks past CAULIFLOWER, and moves toward the MUSCLEMAN.

MAE   Hiya, tall, dark and handsome.

MUSCLEMAN   Oh, Miss West. Pardon me. I'll slip into a robe.

MAE   Never mind. It pays to advertise.

MUSCLEMAN   I hope you're still looking for a Mr. America for your act. I'd certainly like to get the job.

Mae, Red, and Reg Lewis.

CAULIFLOWER (staring at Mae) For goodness sakes, you look like Mae West.

MAE Goodness had nothin' to do with it!

CAULIFLOWER (suddenly ducks for cover)

Oh no! Duck! Duck! Here comes a flock of 'em! Oh, they're peacocks. They must be on their way to that other network for the color programs!

MAE I'd ask you to get lost, but I'm afraid you already are.

MUSCLEMAN Cauliflower, Miss West and I are discussing business. I may be the new Mr. America in her act.

MAE And boy you've got what it takes!

CAULIFLOWER   What about me? What about me?

MAE   It looks like they took what you had!

MUSCLEMAN   Never mind him. I want you to look at these muscles. (He flexes.)

MAE   Oh, terrific. Like Idaho potatoes.

CAULIFLOWER (flexing)

How do you like these potatoes?

Red, Mae, and Reg Lewis.

MAE   Oh. Mashed!

MUSCLEMAN   (flexing and posing) And just look at this, Miss West!

MAE	Oh, you got the job, big boy, come up and see me sometime.
	Scene fades out and fades back into COPELAND interviewing MAE in her living room.
COPELAND	It sounds like an interesting experience.
MAE	All my experiences with men are interesting.
COPELAND	Tell me, which do you like the best? Great big musclemen, intelligent men, or handsome men?
MAE	Yes.
COPEPLAND	Let me rephrase that question. Is there any type of man that doesn't appeal to you?
MAE	The type of man that doesn't appeal to me? Let me think. Oh, there must be. Oh, yes. It's the clumsy type. A clumsy man kind of bothers me. Someone awkward and stumbling and fumbling like a character I once met…
	Scene fades out and fades into a hotel lobby set. CLEM KADIDDLEHOPPER (Skelton) stumbles onto the set dropping luggage.
MAE (V.O.)	…see what I mean.
	CLEM and the hotel MANAGER chat in anticipation of MAE's entrance. The MANAGER orders CLEM to straighten things up and exits. Music swells and MAE enters.

MAE   (looking at the mess at Clem's feet) Hmmm… looks like a missile that fizzled.

CLEM   (straightens himself up and gazes at Mae) Alice in Wonderland… Say, has anybody ever told you you look like Mae West?

MAE   Thanks for the compliment. Did anybody ever tell you you look like Red Skelton?

CLEM   Now! Let's not get insulting about this!

Mae meets Clem Kadiddlehopper.

MAE   Where's the manager? I'd like to talk to him about my suite.

CLEM   Your sweet what?

MAE   Something tells me you are a mature man.

CLEM   Ya.

MAE	What's your name, boy?
CLEM	Boy?! How big do the men grow where you come from? My name is Clem Kadiddlehopper.
MAE	Ah… don't get vulgar.
CLEM	Vulgar Kadiddlehopper is my cousin.
MAE	You must have been put together with a Do It Yourself Kit.
CLEM	Ya. The wrong way.

Mae and Clem.

MANAGER	(enters) Oh, Miss West. I'm sorry to keep you waiting. Clem, get Miss West's luggage quickly.
CLEM	(saluting) Luggage. Ey, ey, sir! Ey, ey!

MANAGER   Why do you keep saying Ey, Ey?

CLEM   Because every time I salute, I put my finger in my Ey, Ey, sir.

MANAGER   Welcome to my hotel, Miss West. I'm delighted you registered with me!

MAE   Well, I want you to know you register with me, too!

MANAGER   (bows and the flower in his lapel flies off with a pop) Oh, thank you, Miss West!

MAE   Don't look now, but you just popped your petals.

MANAGER   Should we go up, Miss West?

MANAGER and MAE step toward the elevator.

Scene Fades out, and fades in – back in MAE's living room with COPELAND still asking questions.

COPELAND   Miss West, you certainly have a great effect on the opposite sex. Tell me what is this hidden power you have over men?

MAE   I didn't know it was hidden!

COPELAND   I'll bet you've had hundreds and hundreds of admirers.

MAE   Confidentially, I know so many men that the FBI calls on me to compare fingerprints.

COPELAND   Tell me, out of all these man you've met, have you ever run across a man who was not trustworthy? I mean a man you couldn't trust?

MAE   Oh, I've met a few D.J.s.

COPELAND   You mean disc jockeys?

MAE   No. Dishonest Joes. But the slickest sharp shooter I ever met was on the Mississippi. He was the captain of a river boat. A big wheel. And his name was HONEST SAN FERNANDO RED.

Scene fades out and fades in to the gambling tables on a riverboat. RED (Skelton) is playing cards and joking with a FRENCHMAN. Music swells as MAE enters.

RED   Wow!

FRENCHMAN   Bonsoir, Madame.

MAE   Hi Frenchy. L'mour toujours. L'mour. I hope you get the message.

RED   I'm not even French, and you're getting through to me.

FRENCHMAN   Madame, I do not advise you to play cards with this man. I think he's crooked.

MAE   Well, maybe I can straighten him out.

RED   Won't you sit down, Ma'am? How about a little game of cards here? What's your pleasure?

MAE   Never mind. Just let's play cards.

RED   Did anybody ever tell you you look like Mae West?

MAE   I *am* Mae West.

RED   I wondered why the ends of my mustache was twitching there. I tell you what we'll do. We'll play a little fast game. Care to cut 'em?

MAE cuts the cards.

Mae and San Fernando Red.

RED   Thank you. We'll play a little draw poker here.

MAE   Ya, but keep your hands out of the drawer!

RED   Yes, sir.

MAE   (picks up a stack of chips laying on the table.)

	I think I'll use this… it's just lying around. I'll open with a hundred. Anything wild?
RED	Not yet, but that perfume is pushing in my direction, I'll tell you that. It smells wonderful. What is that?
MAE	It's my favorite perfume. *Ashes of Men*.
RED	(offering his arm) How do you like this stuff? It's *Rabbit Hutch Number 5*. How many cards do you want?
MAE	I think I like what I got.
RED	So do I. (playing fast and loose with the cards hidden in his pockets and up his sleeve) Since you were the opener, you could have had four, and I need three, so I'll take seven! Ah, I got four aces. What have you got?
MAE	What have I got? 41 – 26, and 38.
RED	Looks like you win!
MAE	(Gathering all the chips on the table.) You've been a doll. A real doll.

Scene fades out.

For the show's finale, Red and Mae took center stage.

Mae and Red prepare to shoot the finale.

RED Miss West, I want to thank you for being on my show tonight. You were wonderful. The producer thought you were wonderful, and the director thought you were wonderful. And we'll find out what the censor thought as soon as we let him out of his straight jacket. Okay, boys! You can let him out now!

A scream is heard off stage, and a loud shot.

MAE You see that! They loved it!

RED By the way, I want to ask you something.

MAE Well, ask me and I promise to tell the truth, the whole truth, and nothin' but the truth so help me Perry Mason.

Red and Mae.

RED	You've always been surrounded by so many men. What is it you have that other girls don't have?
MAE	Why ask? Why don't you come up and see me sometime!
RED	I'd like to ask you something else about that phrase. Why do you think it became so famous?
MAE	When I created the famous character Diamond Lil that was the line she spoke to the Salvation Army Captain. Of course, it was the way she said it and what she did when she said it that

made it so famous. But I think every woman likes a man to come up and see her sometime.

Red and Mae.

RED   In other words, you do like to have a man around the house.

MAE   The most!

                    Music swells and Mae sings "It's So Nice to Have a Man Around the House" with special lyrics, and a group of male backup singers.

                    THE END

Mae sings "It's So Nice to Have a Man Around the House."

Henry Fonda and Mae West promote *Hollywood: The Fabulous Era.*

CHAPTER 9

Mae West and a Talking Horse

*"Honey, they haven't invented
the man who isn't my type."*

NEARLY FOUR YEARS WOULD pass before Mae West appeared on television again. In an interview for *TV Guide* magazine published on February 29, 1964, she actually said that her engagement on *The Red Skelton Show* was less than satisfying. "Red is a slapstick comedian," she opined, "and I have to work a little rougher than I like to in that kind of situation. I don't like to exaggerate my type. I like to keep a regalness, a little insinuation." After her appearance with Skelton in 1960, she had taken a break from the spotlight with the exception of a stock tour in her play, *Sextet*, during the summer of 1961.

Mae proposed co-hosting a TV series with a fictional psychologist named "Dr. Harry H. Hoffman," set in a room in her home that she called her "consultatorium." Based on her enviable life experiences and the knowledge of "Dr. Hoffman," they would solve the problems of everyday life for the "everyday man" in the 30-minute program. Nothing came of her idea.

In the summer of 1962, Mae recorded a single titled, "Am I Too Young." The rock 'n' roll/novelty record featured the voice of a young man and the actress exchanging bon mots. The record was banned from numerous radio stations. In a June 20 interview for the *Los Angeles Herald Examiner*, she told reporter Bob Hull that she wanted to stay active in response to her many young fans' requests.

"They see my movies on television," she said, "the teenagers, you know, and they send me fan mail. They're so wonderful. And they come to see me on the stage! Imagine, kids spending six dollars!"

She said she wasn't particularly surprised to be banned on the radio again. She recalled the time a few years earlier when her recorded appearance on *Person to Person* was cancelled before being broadcast. Since that time, she explained, she avoided the small screen. "I think you can get overexposed on television."

Nevertheless, encouraged by the success of her record and newfound appeal to a young generation, she revealed a plan to produce and star in a cartoon series titled *Pretty Mae*, which would only utilize her voice. Her agent contacted Jack Kinney and asked if he would be interested in working with the actress to develop and animate the series. Kinney had joined the Walt Disney Studio in 1931. He began as an animator and worked on dozens of cartoon shorts and feature animated films before leaving Disney in 1958 to pursue his own projects. He continued to work as an artist, but also became a very successful story editor, director and producer of animated short films. His Hollywood-based company, Jack Kinney Productions, presented many cartoon series including a color version of the classic *Popeye the Sailor* (1960-61). He presented the actress with a *Pretty Mae* synopsis, and more than a dozen hand-colored cartoon cells featuring Mae, and the other characters he crafted for the series.

"There is no doubt," Kinney wrote, "that an Animation Cartoon Television series based on and around the fabulous and fascinating character, style and voice of Miss Mae West will have tremendous appeal as entertainment for all of us – those of us who have enjoyed her performances in the past and the new generation of audience who will be afforded the opportunity to enjoy this very special treat in a new medium.

"The basic concept of the production will always carry with it the awareness of *Pretty Mae* personified as a reigning sex symbol with the gestures and wit that have made her famous – the femme fatale – with a tongue in cheek approach – with an underlying feeling that she is kidding and the whole thing is all in fun.

"*Pretty Mae* will be played as a person who is torn between good and bad – who would like to be bad but cannot because of her overpowering *good* self that always emerges victoriously when in conflict with her *bad* self.

"The *good* self and *bad* self will be depicted as little elves or leprechauns both fighting to influence *Pretty Mae*.

"Lucifer D. Scratch, the Devil himself, will be played very broad as a completely frustrated individual whose diabolical schemes always go astray, thanks to *Pretty Mae* who with the help of her *boys* and *better self* continually louse up Lucifer's best laid plans.

"Lucifer is the screwball demon who when playing with fire always gets burned. He is allergic to fire, and brimstone makes him sneeze. Lucifer's helpers, a motley group of weird creatures, are really no help at all – always bungling in their attempts at wickedness and catching hell from the Devil for their inept assistance.

"*Pretty Mae's* boys – Vitamin, Shortage, Punchy, Freddy the Fink, and others, are gangster types played for comedy – and ever ready to assist and carry out the orders of their fascinatin' lady boss.

Mae with Henry Fonda.

"Binns the Butler, is an Oxford accented reformed conman and a good foil for Prudence the Cockney Maid, a former shop-lifter. The by-play between these two will lend itself to more comedy.

"Fantasy and musical sequences will be introduced wherever possible, and each episode will open and close with *Pretty Mae* singing her theme song."

Kinney worked closely with the actress. In his autobiography, he recalled, "We had story meetings with her at our studio, and even dropped in to see her in her penthouse atop her Ravenswood apartments, in her white and gold bedroom complete with circular bed, mirrored ceiling and pet spider monkeys. She indeed was a real lady. She believed in proper diet, exercise, and no booze or tobacco. She had a delightful personality and a great gag and story sense, very clean dialogue and speech, only innuendo, a real pleasure to work with."

Mae and Henry Fonda pose for photographer John Engstead.

Contract negotiations stalled over who would maintain creative control. Not surprisingly, Kinney could not sell their *Pretty Mae* cartoon proposal. However, in 1965, he successfully tapped into the movie-star theme when he became the story writer for the Saturday morning cartoon series, *The New Three Stooges*.

Later that year, Mae agreed to help promote a television documentary about the history of movies, titled *Hollywood: The Fabulous Era*. Produced by David Wolper, directed by Jack Haley Jr., and hosted by Henry Fonda, the one-hour special, which aired on November 28, 1962, featured film clips of classic films and film stars. Mae West did not appear on camera. Her appearance on the special was limited to film clips from *She Done Him Wrong*, however, she agreed to be photographed with Fonda for print advertisements for the program. The photographs appeared on *TV Guide* covers, and many magazines and newspapers prior to the broadcast.

In 1963, producer Arthur Lubin coaxed Mae back in front of the television cameras. Lubin and the actress were old friends. The two met in 1932 when he worked as an associate producer for William LeBaron at Paramount. Lubin worked on the film *She Done Him Wrong*. The producer was charming, witty and gay; qualities Mae especially appreciated in a man. He was one of only a few "Hollywood" acquaintances she maintained, and he produced the unlikely hit situation comedy, *Mr. Ed*, which starred a talking horse.

The actress and the producer shared an interest in a self-proclaimed psychic named Rev. Thomas Jack Kelly. Lubin was a financial contributor to Kelly's "church" and sponsored his appearances in Southern California. Lubin's many credits included feature films and television programs, but *Mr. Ed* may have been his biggest – and longest lasting – television hit. Lubin told Mae that an appearance on his program would be beneficial to her career because the comedy had a very large and young television audience. He enlisted the aid of Rev. Kelly, who encouraged Mae to accept Lubin's offer.

Announcing
Television's Funniest Moment
when . . . "MAE WEST MEETS MR. ED"
On the "Mister Ed" show over CBS-TV.
September 13, 1964.

Watch your local listings, and mark the date to witness the hilarious encounter between the fabulous Mae West, and television's talking horse.

The Mae West Fan Club promotional postcard for her appearance on *Mr. Ed*.

In the fall of 1963, Lubin presented Mae with a script entitled, "Mae West Meets Mr. Ed," written by two veteran comedy writers, Lou Derman, and Bill Davenport. Mae worked on the script to give it what Lubin called the "Mae West flavor." The episode was filmed on January 13, 14, and 15, 1964 for Filmways TV Productions at General Service Studios at 1040 North Las Palmas Avenue in Hollywood. Mae was treated like royalty on the set, and signed autographs and posed for pictures with the cast and crew, as well as studio office staff members. For the boudoir scenes in the show, she insisted that her own bedroom furniture, including her canopied bed, be moved from her nearby apartment to the production facility.

The cast regulars included Alan Young and Connie Hines as Wilbur and Carol Post, and Leon Ames and Florence MacMichael as the next door neighbors Gordon and Winnie Kirkwood. Alan Young recalled, "Mae West told me that once she made up her mind to make a television appearance, she wanted to work only with the handsomest, biggest and strongest male in the medium. Who else but Mr. Ed?"

Connie Hines remembered, "We were very excited to have Miss West on the show! Arthur was an old friend of hers, and he was very accommodating to her. She had her own clothes and dressers and hair and make-up people and body guard and chauffeur, her own entourage, and even had some of her furniture on the set. She was nice, but I didn't have much interaction with her. I was in just one scene with her. She really didn't want to do scenes with any women. She only wanted to be in publicity photos with Alan."

"I thought she was great," Alan said, "very funny. It was a pleasure to meet her. I saw her on Broadway in *Diamond Lil*. She was fantastic! She flirted and we had a fun time with her. We had other big guest stars, but she was the biggest. Larger than life, and she was tiny in person. She hadn't done much TV, though. I think Arthur begged her to do the show. It was a different style of acting for her, I think. She had worked so much on stage that she was very broad in her delivery and gestures. She was also used to working in front of a live audience. I think she found it a little awkward to deliver her lines and not hear any audience response. Theater actors feed off that, it affects their performance. It threw off her timing a little bit, but we kept at it. She found her rhythm. There were a lot of retakes and a lot of editing later, but the episode was a good one and fans loved it. Everyone loved her on the set. She was pleasant to everybody and very funny naturally. I liked her. Such a presence. She was supposed to come back for another one."

Entertainment reporter Val Adams interviewed Mae over the telephone when she completed filming her guest shot on *Mr. Ed*. She was confined to her apartment for a short time to recover from a secretive stay in the hospital for cataract surgery on both eyes. The interview appeared in the *Los Angeles Times* on January 22, 1964.

Adams asked why she agreed to appear on a television program that had a large, and very youthful, audience.

"It is unusual for me to appear on this kind of show, but I'm doing it to please my fans," she said. "You know, I now have three generations of fans and there are lots of new fan clubs among teenagers."

Mae, Mr. Ed, and Alan Young.

Adams wondered how teenagers had discovered her after being away from films for so many years.

"They saw me with Rock Hudson on the Academy Awards show," she explained. "I got fan mail for two years after that. And they see some of my old pictures on 'The Late Show'."

The actress revealed the storyline for her episode. "I have brought horses from Paris and I call the architect to fix my stables. I want a French décor so they will not become homesick. And I want the stables trimmed in gold to match the horses' hoofs."

The story unfolds when Mae takes an interest in Mr. Ed, based on his sexy telephone voice. Ed runs away from the Post household to live with her pampered horses, but returns contrite, after being subjected to bubble baths, mane and tail braids, and imported cologne.

The actress said, "My fans have written to say they are thrilled I will be on the show. Some say they will invite people in and have viewing parties. I look 26 or 28. My secret is positive thinking and no drinking. I never smoke and I'm health-minded. I eat vegetables, exercise and walk a lot in the sand at my beach house. I'm physically fit at all times."

Adams asked if she intended to make more television appearances.

"They've been trying to get me to do a panel program on which I would do interviews, but I'm not interested in this. My people want me in there in costume and doing my stuff."

Mae granted an extensive interview to reporter Hank Grant, which was printed in *TV TIME Magazine* (and syndicated) on February 7, 1964. The interview occurred in her Santa Monica beach house. Grant wrote, "Mae was dressed in a peach negligee with a delicately laced beige-colored jacket. She still has that dazzling, even-toothed smile and the sloe-eyed look that causes male necks to turn wherever she goes. Even at close range, she looked every bit as young as she did in her last movie, and that was many years ago."

The reporter asked if she was considering a television career.

"You might say Mae West is ready for television," she said, "but is television ready for Mae West? Frankly, I don't like the unhealthy turn television has taken. All because of a hue and cry about excessive violence and sex on TV, producers have eliminated healthy sex and substituted clinical approaches to sex that are morbid and depressing, some are even frighteningly unromantic. Let me support my argument by asking you if you're not tired of medical series that constantly deal with adultery, frigidity, rapists and even sexual deviates.

"Now, I expect some of your readers will sneer and say, 'Look who's setting herself up as a paragon of virtue.' Well, I'm not. What comprises virtue depends on your point of view, but we won't go into that. What is important is that young people should have a healthy attitude toward sex. I became a sex symbol by poking fun at it. Laughter about any serious subject is healthy, but particularly as concerns sex. When you can be calm about sex – smile, even laugh – you're not obsessed with it. It's the obsessed people who cause grave trouble for themselves and others.

"I don't suppose you realize I had as many women fans as men fans. Now, that's something for the number one sex symbol – that's what they called me for some twenty years, and some still do. If you think back to each and every movie I ever made, I played fair with sex. Never once on the screen did I ever steal a man away from his wife. Incidentally, for the record, I never did in my private life, either.

"And adultery was never indicated in any of my pictures. About the hottest scene I ever remember playing was when this eager beaver was smothering me with kisses and I stopped him cold by yawning and saying, 'Honey, peel me a grape.'

"Where TV has become clinically morbid with sex, the stage is unbelievably foul with plays that glorify procurers and prostitutes, deviates and other characters I'd never allow to even be mentioned in any show I'd ever done on the stage or on the screen.

"TV gets away with it by having a surgeon or a psychiatrist furrowing his brows over the problem. The thinking in TV these days seems to be, 'Let's make sex dreadful; instead of a light romantic approach, how can we make it shocking? Let's forget about natural, God-given, healthy happy love and entertain viewers with a show about an abortionist.'

"That's what I mean when I asked is TV ready for Mae West. I haven't changed and I never will. The type of show I would do would poke gentle fun at human weaknesses, but in a way that would make both men and women viewers laugh as one, rather than incite an argument over the respective merits of their genders. Do you think TV is ready for *that*?"

Mae and Alan Young.

To promote Mae's appearance on *Mr. Ed*, Mike Jackson interviewed the actress for the *Los Angeles Herald Examiner* on March 12, 1964. "Way out West," Jackson wrote. "*Mr. Ed*, TV's talking horse, will have a few words with Mae West. The results may be calamitous!" Arthur Lubin told the reporter, "She's incredibly modest, almost shy. She's a real pro and always knows her lines."

Jackson visited Mae at her Santa Monica home. "There's an armed guard at the entrance," he reported. He was ushered into her bedroom for the interview. "The bedroom is a pure stage set," he wrote, "white and gold full mirrors, with a tremendous circular bed beneath a satin and lace canopy. Miss West's companions are two wooly monkeys, 'Baby' and 'Pretty Boy.' They swing on the bars she has set up for them in the play room. Both are TV fans, can turn on the set, and chatter when animals turn up on the screen."

Mae talked about guarding her privacy and her reluctance to do much television. "If too many people see you, you lose your luster," she explained. "When you are a star, you have to love yourself first. Nothing, no sentiment or relationship can break through. I've always given my audience what they want. I wouldn't change one minute of my life."

The premise of "Mae West Meets Mr. Ed" was a case of simple mistaken identity. Mae West hires Wilbur Post to redesign her horse stable, but mistakes Mr. Ed – who answered her phone call on Wilbur's behalf – for the architect's handsome, deep-voiced, personal associate.

Veteran character actor Nick Stewart played the role of Mae's butler. She insisted on using Nick, also known professionally as Nicodemus Stewart, who had appeared in her 1936 film, *Go West Young Man*. A handsome young actor named Jacques Shelton played the part of one of her horse groomsmen. Shelton was the boyfriend of her friend, producer Hunt Stromberg, Jr.

Mae West's scenes as *originally* written – and included here – provided her with more screen time on the *Mr. Ed* episode. Although filmed, her scenes were edited down to showcase the series' cast. When the "Mae West Meets Mr. Ed" episode begins, Mr. Ed is sleeping in his stall in Wilbur Post's barn. The telephone rings, which awakens him.

ED   (to himself) Huh? What's that? Oh, the phone. Okay, okay. Keep your saddle on. I shouldn't have watched that late, late, late, late show last night.

ED knocks the phone off the hook.

ED   Hello?

The scene cuts to Mae West's boudoir.

Mae on the set of her boudoir on *Mr. Ed*.

MAE	Hello. Is this Mr. Post?
ED	No, I'm his associate… who is this, please?
MAE	My name is Mae West.
ED	Mae West! Are you Mae West, that great motion picture star?
MAE	Let's put it this way, honey. I certainly am.
ED	I've seen your movies on TV. Gee! Golly! Oh, boy! Wow!
MAE	That was my movie all right. I'm thinking of having my stables remodeled. Is Mr. Post free to take the job?
ED	When would you want him to start?
MAE	Immediately. Tell him I'm a lady who can't wait.
ED	Well, he's got a lot of work, but I guess he can squeeze you in.
MAE	Sounds delightful… Is Mr. Post married?
ED	Oh, yes.
MAE	You have an interesting voice… are you married?
ED	No, but I'm not your type.
MAE	Honey, they haven't invented the man who isn't my type.
ED	Uh… I'm not exactly a man.
MAE	What are you? A monkey?

Mae on the set of *Mr. Ed*.

ED   No. But you're in the right category.

MAE   Tell Mr. Post I'd like to stop by at seven tonight. I'll be passing by on my way to a PTA meeting.

ED   PTA?

MAE   That's right. I'm giving a talk on physical fitness. Would you care to hear it?

ED   Umm… no, thanks. I'm in great shape. I run over a hundred miles a week.

MAE   My. You must be as strong as a horse.

ED   I'll go along with that… well, goodbye, Miss West.

	ED replaces the phone in the cradle. Scene cuts to Mae's boudoir. MAE hangs up the telephone.
MAE	Goodbye, whatever you are! Not a man, and not a monkey! Sounds like a cool cat!
	Scene cuts to Wilbur's barn.
ED	(to himself) Mae West… maybe she can come up and shoe me sometime.
	WILBUR enters the barn and scolds ED for keeping such a messy stall. ED tells WILBUR that Mae West wants to hire him to design her horse stalls, and that she will drop by that evening. WILBUR hurries out to tell, Carol, his wife. ED commiserates to himself and contemplates running away from home to a place where he won't be constantly nagged.
	Scene cuts to a limousine parked in front of the Post's house. A uniformed chauffeur opens the rear door, and MAE WEST is ushered out of the car by two strapping young men dressed in top hats and tails.
MAE	All right, boys. Be back in ten minutes. Believe it or not, I've gotta see a man about a barn.
	MAE walks to the Post's front door, and rings the bell. CAROL POST opens the door excitedly.
CAROL	Hello, Miss West. I'm Mrs. Post. Please come in.

Mae on the set.

MAE	(offers a card from her purse) My calling card…
CAROL	(looks at the card which is the queen of hearts from a deck of playing cards) The Queen of hearts!
MAE	Thanks very much.
	CAROL ushers MAE into the living room. WILBUR rushes over to them.
WILBUR	Well, hello, Miss West! This certainly is a pleasure! I'm Wilbur Post and I see you've met my wife.
CAROL	Won't you sit down?

Mae meets Carol Post.

MAE	Honey, in this gown, you don't dare sit down… it's standing room only.

WILBUR	I know you've only got a few minutes, Miss West, so why don't we step out to my office? This way please.

	As they approach the patio door, the Post's next door neighbor WINNIE comes in carrying a pot.

WINNIE	Carol, I was just washing the dishes when I remembered I borrowed this saucepan. Oh, I'm sorry. I didn't know you had company.

WILBUR	Miss West, I'd like you to meet our neighbor, Mrs. Kirkwood.

WINNIE	It's a pleasure Miss West! My, you look stunning. How do you manage to keep yourself so young… so glamorous?

MAE	Positive thinking and no drinking. Proper diet... and lie about your age.
CAROL	We've all heard so much about you, Miss West!
MAE	I know... but you can't prove it.
WILBUR	Well, I know you're in a hurry, Miss West, so if you'll just step out to my office.
	WILBUR escorts MAE to the doorway when their neighbor, Winnie's husband GORDON, arrives formally dressed in a military uniform decorated with ribbons and medals.
GORDON	Wilbur, I was on my way to... Oh, I hope I'm not interrupting anything.
WILBUR	Miss West, I'd like you to meet Colonel Kirkwood. I believe he has a speech prepared for you.
GORDON	Oh, it's not a speech. Just a few words.
WINNIE	Gordon, why are you wearing your soldier's suit?
GORDON	Well, uh, I was on my way to an Air Force Reserve meeting...
CAROL	I thought that meeting was next week.
WILBUR	Nothing like getting an early start to beat that freeway traffic.
MAE	I'm sorry I didn't recognize you, Colonel. You haven't changed a bit... my, you look distinguished. I've always admired men in uniform.

GORDON	You have?!
MAE	I get choked up when I see a good humor man!
WILBUR	Well, I know you're in a hurry, Miss West, so if you'll just step out to my office…
CAROL	Just one question, Miss West… if you won't consider it embarrassing…
MAE	I don't mind embarrassing questions if you don't mind embarrassing answers.
CAROL	Well… do you have any beauty secrets you might let us in on?
MAE	Like I'm going to tell those ladies at the PTA… you've got to be feminine… dress like a woman, look like a woman, act like a woman, feel like a woman… that's what separates the men from the girls.
WILBUR	That is so true. Whenever Carol puts on a pair of slacks, she looks…
CAROL	She looks what?
WILBUR	Beautiful!

WILBUR takes MAE's arm and starts to lead her away.

WILBUR	I know you're in a hurry, Miss West, so if you'll come with me to the barn.
MAE	To the barn?!

WILBUR   That's where my office is.

MAE   Naturally.

            The scene cuts to the interior of the barn. WILBUR is taking copious notes. Mr. Ed's stall door is closed.

WILBUR   Now, then, Miss West, just how much remodeling do you want done on your stable?

MAE   Quite a bit. I bought these horses in Paris… so I'd like the barn designed in French Provincial.

WILBUR   French Provincial barn?

MAE   Yes, it'll keep the horses from getting homesick.

WILBUR   Oh… yes… now, do you have any ideas for the interior?

MAE   I'd like a French décor… plus air conditioning… unit heat… acoustical ceiling… mural wallpaper and a roll-away feedbox.

WILBUR   Rollaway feedbox?

MAE   With a built-in moisturizer to keep the hay fresh and crisp.

WILBUR   Very smart. There's nothing worse than starting off the day with a mouthful of stale hay.

MAE   Then I'd like louvre windows… stereophonic music… overhead sun lamps, and a tuck-away tack room.

WILBUR   Tuck-away tack room?

MAE   When not in use, it'll swing into the wall… keep the saddles and bridles out of sight.

WILBUR   I see. Kind of make them forget they're beasts of burden.

MAE   Exactly. As I was telling your associate…

WILBUR   Associate?

MAE   Yes, the one with the deep, masculine voice.

    WILBUR realizes she had spoken with Mr. Ed on the phone.

WILBUR   Oh.

MAE   I'd like to meet him sometime. He sounds like a man about town.

WILBUR   Well, you could say he knows his oats.

MAE   Oh, likes to horse around, hmmm?

WILBUR   Miss West, don't you think your stable might be a little too pretentious?

MAE   Oh, no, horses are among my favorite creatures.

WILBUR   Mine, too. I'd never go horseback riding without one.

MAE   I don't ride my horses, Mr. Post.

WILBUR   You don't? Then… what do you do with them?

MAE   I lavish them in the lap of luxury.

The scene cuts to the inside of Mr. Ed's stall, where he's been listening at the door to the conversion. He mumbles to himself.

MR. ED   If horses ever get the vote, she'll be our first Lady President.

Later, WILBUR argues with MR. ED who still hasn't cleaned his dirty stall. He scolds the horse and punishes him by taking away his television set until he properly cleans his mess. Exasperated, Mr. Ed decides to run away.

The scene cuts to Mae West's entry hall. The doorbell rings and CHARLES, the butler, opens the door and is shocked to see MR. ED standing on the doorstep with a large bonnet on his head. A sign hangs from around his neck. CHARLES turns and calls out.

CHARLES   Miss… Miss West… come!

MAE WEST enters and stops abruptly when she sees MR. ED standing in the foyer.

MAE   What's that horse doing here?

CHARLES   I… I don't know!

CHARLES reaches for the sign and reads it aloud.

CHARLES   It says, "Dear Miss West, I am leaving my little horsie on your doorstep. You can give him the care I cannot afford. Please give my baby a good home and the love he needs. Bless you. Signed, Desperate Mother!"

Mae reunited with actor Nick Stewart.

MAE	Oh, poor little fella. Charles, get the guest stall ready. We've got an orphan in the family.

Meanwhile, WILBUR has discovered that Mr. Ed is missing, and he calls the police.

The scene cuts to the lavish interior of Mae West's barn at night. MR. ED is standing in a large tub taking a bubble bath. He is wearing a large frilly shower cap. MAE is supervising the bath. MR. ED is attended to by two handsome groomsmen, who are both soaked in water and bubbles.

MAE	Scrub him down good, boys. I don't want him to smell like a horse… Make him look sleek and chic.

MR. ED flicks his tail and bubbles splash one of the groomsmen in the face.

GROOMSMAN #1   Hey, watch it!

MAE   What's the matter, Paul?

Mr. Ed takes a bath.

GROOMSMAN #1   I don't think he likes his bubble bath.

GROOMSMAN #2   He's been bathing us more than we've been bathing him!

MAE   He's just a playful baby. Aren't you, tall, blond and bushy-tailed?

The groomsmen brush out Ed's coat as MAE watches.

MAE   Brush a little harder, boys. I want his coat to look like a full-length mink.

The groomsmen brush harder.

MR. ED   Ouch!

Mae with Mr. Ed.

GROOMSMAN #1 braids ED's tail with colorful ribbons. GROOMSMAN #2 files one of ED's hoofs. MAE watches.

MAE   Braid his tail nice and tight. I hate a horse with a sloppy hair-do.

GROOMSMAN #1 braids the tail a little tighter, and ED groans. MAE picks up a large atomizer.

MAE   Nothing like a little French perfume. I always say, promise a horse anything, but give him perfume!

MAE sprays ED with the atomizer, and he loudly sneezes.

GROOMSMAN #2   He sneezed!

MAE   Give him a tissue.

GROOMSMAN #1   Think he's catching a cold, Miss West?

MAE   Better check his pulse. And take his temperature.

GROOMSMAN #1   Pulse? Where can I find his pulse?

Publicity photo of Mae and Mr. Ed.

MAE   In his wrist, of course! Never mind. Call the vet and have him give all the vitamin shots from A to Z.

MR. ED's ears prick up at the mention of vitamin shots and needles.

GROOMSMAN #1   Gee, this horse seems very nervous. You think that needle might scare him?

MAE   A few shots a day won't hurt him. After all, horses sleep standing up.

Mae with Mr. Ed and his trainer, Lester Hilton.

Later that evening, Wilbur is in the barn and speaks about Ed's disappearance to the police on the phone. Suddenly he hears the sound of Mr. Ed's clapping hoofs. WILBUR informs the police that Ed is back, and hangs up the phone. Mr. Ed complains about all the pampering he received at Mae's house. He tells WILBUR he is so happy to be back that he will now clean his stall.

Mae West

Mae talks with Mr. Ed on the phone.

Moments later, WILBUR is scrubbing the perfume off the horse.

MR. ED   Keep scrubbing, Wilbur. I can still smell the perfume. Iccchh.

WILBUR   So… you weren't too happy at Mae West's house, huh?

MR. ED   It's a very nice place to visit, but I wouldn't want to live there.

	Suddenly, the telephone rings. WILBUR picks up the receiver.
WILBUR	Hello? Oh, hi Miss West. Yes, I've sketched out some ideas and I'd like to bring them by this afternoon.
	Scene cuts to the beautiful interior of Mae's bedroom.
MAE	I know what a busy man you must be, Mr. Post. Why don't you have your associate drop them by?
WILBUR	My associate?
MAE	The one with the deep interesting voice. May I speak to him for a moment?
	WILBUR holds the phone out to MR. ED.
WILBUR	Ed, Miss West wants to talk to you.
	He holds the phone so the horse can speak.
MR. ED	Hello? Gee, I'd like to come over, but I have a previous appointment.
MAE	Couldn't you break it? Who is the appointment with?
MR. ED	The U.S. Army. I've just been drafted!
	Scene cuts to the interior of Mae's bedroom. She hangs up the phone, and sighs.
MAE	It's no use. I just gotta start my own draft board…

Mae chats on the telephone with Mr. Ed.

Mae's guest-starring appearance on *Mr. Ed* was a ratings bonanza. She was immediately invited to return in the fall of 1964. A script was prepared, titled "Mae Goes West," which featured the actress calling upon Wilbur again to approve his proposed addition to her stables. During their conversation about their love of horses, Wilbur tells a story about a horse that was responsible for the Gold Rush in California. The rest of the program was a comedic flashback set in the gold rush town of Sutter's Mill in the 1850s. Mae would have played the character of Lady Belle who owns a gambling casino. Before the actress could undertake work on the project, however, she fell ill and was hospitalized in early October. The press speculated that she had suffered a heart attack, some Hollywood columnists supposed she was having cosmetic surgery, but in fact, she was diagnosed with Type 1 Diabetes. She would require a carefully regulated diet, and insulin, for the rest of her life.

On November 3, 1964, Mae's secretary of more than thirty years, Larry Lee, wrote to the actress' friend and longtime fan, Dolly Dempsey, who lived in San Diego. He informed Dolly that Mae would finally be released from Cedars-Sinai Hospital on November 4. "She is feeling pretty good and with a few months rest and keeping herself free of business activities and assorted aggravations, as prescribed by her doctor, she should be completely her healthy, vital self again," he wrote. "Unfortunately, I have some sad news to report – news which couldn't be disclosed to Mae until two weeks after the occurrence. Her brother, John, passed away on October 12. This has been a hell of a year for Mae, and I know we all hope and pray that 1965 will be far happier for her in every way."

Earlier in 1964, Mae's companion, former muscleman Paul Novak, moved out of her home and contemplated re-joining the Merchant Marine. The couple had lived together since 1955, but Mae's brother and sister resented his presence and ever increasing influence over their sister. They bitterly argued with him and Mae, until finally driving Paul to temporarily leave.

It would take a couple of years for Mae to completely recover, and change her diet, eating habits, and exercise regime. Paul Novak helped her get back in shape. He was a good cook, and carefully nursed her back to health.

Mae still received film and television offers. Arthur Lubin was so enthusiastic about her television potential he proposed a situation comedy, tentatively titled *Mae West, Private Detective*. Nothing came of the idea. In 1964, she turned down an episode of *Burke's*

Law titled "Who Killed Vaudeville?" The program featured many old-time vaudevillians. Gloria Swanson accepted the role of "Miss Lily Boles" intended for Mae. The following year she rejected a *Gilligan's Island* script titled "Erika Tiffany-Smith to the Rescue." The script concerned a rich heiress who considers buying "Gilligan's island" to develop an exclusive resort. Zsa Zsa Gabor played the role in the episode broadcast in December, 1965. Producer Nick Vanoff and ABC-TV executives courted the actress to make a special appearance on the new, hit variety show, *Hollywood Palace*, in 1966. Negotiations failed to secure her participation.

A few months after her release from the hospital, Dwight Whitney interviewed the actress for the February 27, 1965 issue of *TV Guide*. The reporter spoke with Mae at her Santa Monica home. "Mae lives on the beach in Santa Monica," he wrote. "Her eight-bedroom house, replete with butler, cook, chauffeur, clerical staff and Cadillac limousine, is early 1930s modern, the style of architecture which resembled the outside of an icebox. Inside all trace of the workaday world vanishes. I fight my way through a forest of crystal and gilt, antique mirrors and candelabra that might look gaudy at Versailles."

Mae told him that she still wanted to do another *Mr. Ed* episode. "My fans liked the other so well," she said, "I was forced to."

She estimated that she had turned down dozens of movie and TV offers in the last ten years. "Because they are not right for me," she stated. "They are not Mae West." She told Whitney that she was busy editing a book about extrasensory perception with her friend Rev. Kelly, rewriting her new *Mr. Ed* script, and writing a novel based on her 1927 play, *The Drag*, which dealt with homosexuality. She also told the reporter that famed movie director George Cukor wanted to make a movie in which she would star as a phony clairvoyant.

Cukor considered several film projects with the actress. He said, "A woman doesn't become a great big personality like that by accident. For all the boldness, there is a certain discretion. No real vulgarity, but only the wit and twinkle of an amusing mind."

Mae said she was never very interested in television because of the many censorship restrictions. She was not impressed with the way women were most often portrayed. Whitney asked her how she felt about family situation comedies like *The Donna Reed Show*. "Donna who?" she wondered.

She said she hoped to do two TV "spectaculars" each year. "I'm waiting for pay-TV," she said. "I'll bet I'll rate number one on it!"

Mae did appear on Canadian television in a fashion in 1965. Veteran Canadian comedy duo Johnny Wayne and Frank Shuster (Wayne & Shuster) hosted a summer series for CBS-Toronto. The one-hour documentary/comedy specials saluted classic movie comedy stars. Wayne & Shuster were popular radio, TV, and film stars in their own right, and were best known to American television audiences for their many appearances on *The Ed Sullivan Show*. *Wayne & Shuster Take an Affectionate Look at Mae West* was broadcast in Canada in 1965. Mae West did not actually appear on the special, which featured archival footage of the star.

Gossip columnist Joyce Haber interviewed Mae for the *Los Angeles Times* on July 31, 1968. Plans were announced for the actress' first television special, *A Night With Mae West*, to be broadcast in September.

"I never liked the idea of doing television," Mae said, "because people could turn me off."

Cary Grant and Gregory Peck were slated to guest star on the show, which was to be produced by *The Sound of Music* director,

Robert Wise. Mae joked, "Going from Julie Andrews to Mae West – he's certainly versatile!" Universal Studios and her publicist, Stanley Musgrove, were set to co-produce.

When Mae called Cary to ask if he'd appear with her, he told her, "Nothing would please me more." Peck said, "I'd be tickled to death."

Mae in 1967.

Plans for Mae West's first color television special dragged on for months. A script was approved, and designers completed sketches of the elaborate sets proposed for the program. Musical numbers were readied, and Edith Head worked on costumes for the actress, but after nearly a year of work, *A Night With Mae West* was shelved. Bigger things were in store for the actress.

In 1970, she would make her triumphant, though controversial, return to the big screen with her role in *Myra Breckinridge*.

Mae's publicity tour for the film took her back to New York City in June of that year – her first visit there in fifteen years. The premiere of *Myra Breckinridge* and the long-awaited return of the seventy-seven-year old sex symbol garnered worldwide news coverage.

Edith Efron interviewed Mae in her suite at the Sherry Netherland Hotel on Friday afternoon, June 26. The interview appeared in the August 22, 1970 issue of *TV Guide*, with the headline, "'Television should be censored!' So says that little old sexpot, Mae West."

Mae unexpectedly expounded on the need for TV censorship. Efron was a bit perplexed, considering that the purpose of the interview was to promote Mae's latest film, which was rated "X" by the Motion Picture Board.

"TV *should* be censored!" Mae stated. "You can't have those *awful* new sex movies on TV. It's *repulsive*. You can get *sick to your stomach* watching them. Sex has to have the greatest *love* behind it to mean anything. Today, sex is like *nothing*! It has no more value – it's a bunch of *animals* out there!

"And the four letter words in these movies! TV is *right* to censor them! Why, you couldn't *pay* me to say those words! TV should stay just the way it is and keep this kind of thing off the air. Because you've got children listening, and a lot of people who live very *properly*. If you didn't have them, the world would go to *pieces* in no time. You've got to have *some* people with dignity. So I think TV should stay that way. *Something* should stay that way! I had *dignity*! My approach to sex was *regal*!

"It's like the old burlesque," she continued. "It was the *scum* of the theater. That isn't *sex* that's going on today. It's *nudity*. If you have a real *sex personality*, you can keep all your clothes *on*.

I was often covered up from my ankles to my neck. *They* take all their clothes off, because they *don't* have *sex personalities*. They've got nothing else to offer but nudity.

"And that is why I'm for keeping these kind of things off TV. When you get right down to it, there are things people just shouldn't be asked to see."

She said she was still planning a television special, and expecting a confrontation with censors. Censorship battles dated back to the zenith of her film career. "The churches said I was corrupting people's morals! They wouldn't let me say all kinds of things. You know what I finally did? I put in absolutely *terrible* lines, on purpose – just to the give the censors something to cut out! It was the only way I could outsmart them!

"Ultimately, they discovered that it didn't really matter what I *said*, it was the *sex personality* itself. It was the way I said it. Once long ago, I made a *Person to Person* on CBS. They never showed it. They said it was too suggestive. They came up to my apartment. It's Louis XIV, all white and gold. There's a marble statue of me on the piano. They said, 'It looks like Venus.' I said, 'Yeah, but I've got arms'."

Paul Novak, also in the hotel suite, prompted her to tell the reporter about the affairs.

"Oh, yeah," she said. "They asked me what I thought about foreign affairs. I said, 'I'm all for 'em'.

"Actually, I don't know *why* they didn't put it on the air. I really didn't say anything too much. I just make things *appear* sexy. Anything I say, they read a double meaning into it."

She dismissed the sexual appeal of women who were then appearing on television, calling them "amusing, pretty, attractive, or interesting," but not "sexy." The reporter asked her if not one woman on TV was sexy.

"If they are sexy," Mae said, "they are not allowed to show it. That is assuming, of course, that they *had* it and *could* show it. Personally, I think it's something they just haven't *got*."

Mae told the reporter that she didn't watch much TV. "That is," she said, "I watch some things. Only I forget what they are. Some kind of detective. And that show with all those men." She then asked Paul to remind her what programs she enjoyed.

"*Perry Mason*," he said, "*Sullivan*, and *Bonanza*. And the news."

"That's right," she said. "Lots of news shows. I watch Walter Cronkite and those men columnists."

Publicity photo of Mae with Mr. Ed.

Mae West on the set of *Myra Breckinridge*, 1969.

CHAPTER 10

Armed Forces Radio Service Christmas Show

"Personally, I prefer a man out
of uniform… the faster the better."

IN 1970, RADIO HOST Frank Bresee interviewed Mae West in her home for his *Golden Days of Radio* program, which aired on the Armed Forces Radio Network. The successful nostalgia radio show was broadcast from 1967 to 1995. Several months later, Bresee and the actress recorded a scripted program, borrowing many one-liners from her films, which became part of the annual Armed Forces Radio Service Christmas Show, broadcast in December, 1971. A second holiday show was edited from the original recordings, and broadcast in December, 1972.

THE MAE WEST CHRISTMAS SHOW 1971

FRANK   And now, the moment you've all been waiting for. Here's that international, sinsational, sexsational, Miss Mae West

MAE   Hmmm... thank you, Frank.

FRANK   Mae, welcome to this special 1971 Christmas Show for our American forces around the world. Mae, since the last time we were on a show together, I've heard a lot about you.

MAE   Ya? But you can't prove it.

FRANK   What I mean is, everyone knows that you're the most renowned personality in the world. A legend in your own time.

MAE   Yes, I know. I climbed the ladder of success wrong by wrong. Just tell me about my future, you see I know all about my past.

FRANK   Mae, while you're here, is there something I can do for you?

MAE   Well, I don't know yet.

FRANK   Well, do you mind if I get a bit personal?

MAE   Go right ahead. I don't mind if you get familiar.

FRANK   Tell me, do you believe in love at first sight?

MAE   I don't know, Frank. But it sure saves a lot of time.

FRANK Mae, do you mind if I ask you just what type of men do you prefer?

MAE Oh, just two types. Foreign and domestic.

FRANK Well, there's no doubt about it. You're a lady that's gotta be handled with kid gloves.

MAE Kid gloves, shoes, stockin's, furs and a couple of diamond lavaliers thrown in.

FRANK Well, you must lead an exciting life.

MAE Yes, Frank, I do. But for a long time, I was ashamed of the way I lived.

FRANK You mean to say you reformed?

MAE No. I just got over being ashamed.

FRANK Well, that's telling it like it is. I guess the devil never made you do anything.

MAE No. When I'm caught between two evils, I generally like to pick the one I never tried before.

FRANK Well, Mae. This is the Christmas season, and the song you do about Santa Claus is one of my favorites.

MAE I love Santa Claus. Beards were always my weakness.

FRANK Do you really mean that?

MAE Hmmm… and besides that, I like the way he slides down my chimney.

FRANK	Well, since this is the Christmas season, do you have a wish for all the fellas listening?
MAE	You mean all those strong, healthy, able-bodied men?
FRANK	Yes, I do.
MAE	I just hope they'll stay strong, healthy, and able-bodied.
FRANK	Well, tell me, what do you think of our men in uniform?
MAE	Frank, personally, I prefer a man out of uniform. The faster the better.
FRANK	There's one thing about being in uniform. While you're serving your country, you have an opportunity to study with the United States Armed Forces Institute, U.S.A.F.I.
MAE	Education is a great thing. I don't know what I'd do without mine. Knowledge ain't so easy to get. You've got to work hard and study. I'm still studyin'. My favorite subject is arithmetic. I was pretty good at figures.
FRANK	Well, Mae, how would you explain addition?
MAE	Addition is when you take one thing and add it to another, and you get two. Two and two is four. And five will get you ten if you know how to work it.
FRANK	How would you explain subtraction?

MAE   Subtraction? Well, that's very simple. For instance, a man has a hundred dollars and you leave him with two. Boy, that's subtraction.

FRANK   Well, no one could explain it like that, Mae. You were wonderful on our Christmas show. I'll never forget you.

MAE   Hmmm… no one ever does.

FRANK   Do you have a Christmas message for the men listening around the world?

MAE   I always have a message for men, 'course it isn't always a Christmas message.

FRANK   Well, how about this Christmas of 1971?

MAE   This Christmas? I want to wish everyone around the world a very Merry Christmas and a Happy New Year. And I hope that the peace for which we're all yearning will become a reality.

FRANK   Thank you, Mae. You were wonderful tonight.

MAE   Frank, I'm always wonderful at night. And if there's ever a day you don't have anything to do and plenty of time to do it, why don't cha come up and see me sometime. Anytime. I'll tell your fortune.

THE END

THE MAE WEST CHRISTMAS SHOW 1972

FRANK   Ladies and gentlemen, it's my particular honor to have in the studio with me one of the greatest personalities of our time. She's an American institution. A star of stars. There's simply nothing like her in the world. Ladies and gentlemen... Miss Mae West!

MAE   Hmmm... thank you, Frank.

FRANK   Mae, welcome to our show.

MAE   It's nice to be here. I like the way the studio's constructed. Come to think of it, I like the way you're constructed, too.

FRANK   Well, it's just light construction.

MAE   Well, turn the light off.

FRANK   Do you have a wish for all the fellas listening?

MAE   You mean all those strong, healthy, able-bodied men?

FRANK   Yes.

MAE   I just hope they'll stay strong, healthy and able-bodied.

FRANK   You know, this show does reach millions of servicemen. That's just a round figure.

MAE   Please, let's not talk of figures. Unless it's mine.

FRANK   Very well, then. What do you think of our men in uniform?

MAE   Hmmm… I like men in uniform. But personally, I prefer a man out of uniform. The faster the better.

FRANK   Well, you know, there's a kind of uniform for women in America at this moment. I'm sure you're aware of the great controversy over the midi, the mini, and the maxie dresses.

MAE   Oh, I've heard of it. In fact, I wear them myself.

FRANK   Then Mae, would you call yourself a liberated woman?

MAE   I never call myself.

FRANK   Well, let me put it another way. What do you think of the Women's Liberation Movement?

MAE   Oh, I'm for it. I'm for any movement.

FRANK   Well, you know the servicemen that are now hearing your voice are on active duty.

MAE   That's the best kind of duty.

FRANK   And they're stationed half way around the world. Right now, for instance, we're being heard in many foreign lands. Do you speak any foreign language?

MAE   Yes, I speak two languages. English and Body.

FRANK   I think a lot of our servicemen speak body English, too. It's sort of an International Language. By the way, what do you think of our servicemen?

MAE   Oh, I like 'em. The enlisted men have the vitality and the officers have the experience.

FRANK	What about the generals?
MAE	Generally speaking, I love the generals. But I have one favorite general.
FRANK	Who's that?
MAE	General Motors!
FRANK	Well, you know, Mae, this is our Special Christmas Show. What about Christmas itself? Do you have Santa Claus at your house?
MAE	You mean the guy that comes down my chimney? I never keep any man out of my house.
FRANK	And the Christmas Spirit? Do you feel it?
MAE	Do I feel it? Oh, I feel it all year.
FRANK	What about a Christmas message for the men listening?
MAE	I always have a message for men… 'course, it isn't always a Christmas message.
FRANK	Well, how about this Christmas?
MAE	This Christmas, I want to wish each and every man listening to my voice a very Merry Christmas and a Happy New Year. I hope you'll soon be home with your loved ones. And if you don't have a loved one… come up and see me sometime! Anytime. I'll tell your fortune.
FRANK	Thank you very much, Miss Mae West!

THE END

CHAPTER 11

Dick Cavett's Backlot USA

"This is the kind of room
I always liked, wall-to-wall men."

TV Guide advertisement for *Dick Cavett's Backlot USA*.

Dick Cavett made numerous overtures through the years to interview Mae West on television. Finally, in February 1976, the two met and discussed his idea to include her in a TV special showcasing four movie legends. *Backlot USA* would include John Wayne, Mickey Rooney, and Gene Kelly. The special would be co-produced by her publicist, Stanley Musgrove. Musgrove negotiated a producer credit in exchange for delivering Mae West. Cavett proposed a fifteen-minute segment that would include an interview, and a musical performance by the actress. At Musgrove's urging, she accepted Cavett's offer of $25,000 for the segment.

The on-camera interview was scheduled to be taped on February 23 at nearby Paramount Studios. Mae balked when the producer refused to provide the interview questions to her beforehand. "I don't work his way," she complained. "I want to see the questions so I can be prepared. And remember, I been around a lot longer than he has." Despite her protestations, the producer held firm.

It took Cavett more than two hours to tape Mae's interview. A small set with a couch and chair and decorated with flowers was positioned in a corner of the otherwise empty, massive soundstage 14 on the Paramount lot. Many of her films were shot there in the 1930s. The interview would eventually be edited down to little more than ten minutes. Cavett said, "You'll see an intelligent woman who's been able to bring off this tremendous character."

At Mae's insistence, Edith Head designed the costumes for the show. "Now this is real nostalgia for me," Edith said. "She created the whole Mae West image herself, and it's the only image in the entire world of stage, screen and television I can think of that's been preserved intact. You see, there still can be magic."

Mae with Dick Cavett.

A few days later, Mae returned to Paramount to tape the musical production numbers for the show. Wearing a black crepe gown and black velvet feathered hat, she sang "Frankie and Johnny" to a playback while walking through a bordello-red, Victorian style saloon and gambling hall. The set was crowded with fifty male extras in appropriate costume, including *Playgirl* magazine's current nude male centerfold, Canadian footballer Lou Zivkovich. Before she began singing, and wending her way through the men seated at tables, she surveyed the crowd, and said, "This is the kind of room I always liked, wall-to-wall men."

Mae sings "Frankie and Johnny" for *Dick Cavett's Backlot USA.*

"She was a little forgetful," choreographer Marc Breaux recalled. Many takes were required. The crew was appreciative and respectful of the star. Breaux said, "They just had to accommodate her, which they were glad to do. Because after you'd worked with her, you became very protective. She was more than a legend. She was something else!"

Mae performs for the television cameras.

Breaux had choreographed many films including *Mary Poppins*, *Sound of Music*, *The Happiest Millionaire*, and *Chitty Chitty Bang Bang*. He recalled working for the Cavett special. "I did a television show with Mae and she did 'Frankie and Johnny,' at Paramount. I'll set the stage a little. There was a long stairway on one side and a roulette table and a dollar wheel and a few arches and a bar. And I wanted her to go from the start of the stairs to the one table and then the next and the next and end up on a little stage in the back.

Mae, poised and ready to go.

"I said, 'Miss West, if you could make your entrance coming down the stairs.' She says, 'I can do anything.' I said, 'When you get down to the bottom step you start the song.' So she came down to the bottom step, started 'Frankie and Johnny.' And that's about a five-minute number – she sang the whole thing before I could stop her and say, you know, 'I just wanted you to do eight bars and then to the roulette table and then you do the second eight, the lyrics to that…' She started there at the roulette table, and sang the song again. And then did the whole thing five times, until she finally ended up on the stage.

Mae sings "After You've Gone".

"Then she was going to do 'After You've Gone.' I said, 'On this number just do whatever you've done before.' And one thing she did I *know* no choreographer could have planned!" At the conclusion of the song, Mae challenged the censors by caressing herself in a suggestive manner.

After completing her finale, she huddled in her dressing trailer with Paul Novak and reporter Kevin Thomas. She told Thomas that she hoped her last "moves" would get past the censors. "I think it's time they laid off me," she said. "After all, I had my clothes on."

Later that evening at dinner at her favorite downtown Chinese restaurant Man Fook Low, she explained to Kevin Thomas, "It wasn't Cavett, it was the Morris office – and, of course, Stan Musgrove – who got me to do it. And it's been such fun to do. That guy, Marc, the choreographer, is great to work with because with him it comes from the heart.

"Gee, this brings back so many happy memories, working at Paramount again. They brought me out at $5,000 a week for the first picture, then they gave me $350,000 a picture plus $100,000 for the script, and $30,000 a week overtime. Once we ran two weeks over and I didn't take it because I thought it had been my fault. They almost dropped dead!"

The party then moved to her Ravenswood apartment. After changing into a more comfortable outfit, she entertained her guests with talk about her just-announced next feature film, *Sextette*. She reminisced about prize fighters and about her time in jail in 1927 for refusing to close down her Broadway show, *Sex*. "It was worth a million dollars in publicity," she said, "and the warden fell in love with me, and even Sir Thomas Lipton came to visit."

She then told a funny story about a questionable jewel dealer who tried to sell her a cheap zircon for $10,000. He actually smuggled star sapphires into the country by feeding them to his dog!

The party broke up at 1:30 in the morning. As her guests were leaving, she said, "I could do two more shows right now! I really could!"

Mae and Dick Cavett meet the press.

A week before the special aired, CBS-TV released a news brief promoting the return of Mae West to television.

"Even though she claims she doesn't really understand women's lib, Mae West struck a blow for women years ago when she began to consult them about their reactions to her performances.

"She recalled this, and other incidents of her colorful career, during taping of her guest appearance on *Dick Cavett's Backlot USA*, an hour-long special dedicated to the era of the big movies, to be broadcast Monday, April 5 (10:00 – 11:00 pm, ET) on the CBS Television Network.

"'I noticed there were always lots more men than women in my audiences,' recalled the inimitable Miss West. 'Now that's fine as far as it goes, but any business person knows you gotta get the support of the women because they often choose the entertainment.'

"So, when women would come backstage to meet her, Miss West would quiz them on what they liked and disliked about the shows.

"'I decided to do shows that would appeal to women as well as men,' she said. 'The women didn't approve of scantily-dressed chorus girls. So I put my girls in long, clinging gowns – and uncovered my musclemen.'

"She also gave women a regal fashion show with each play, interpreting the showy styles in elegant fabrics, floating feathers, and lots of jewelry.

"'I was always famous for what I wore, not for what I didn't wear,' Miss West emphasized. 'I was interested in clothes from the time I was a child and used to window-shop in Brooklyn. I'd look at myself in the store mirrors and try to imagine me in all the fancy gowns.'

"Long fascinated by the fashions of the Gay Nineties, Miss West turned that interest into one of the great characterizations of her career – *Diamond Lil*.

"'The women loved it, and we started a whole style trend,' she recalled. 'They broke away from that skinny, flat-as-a-board look of the Twenties, and began to let their curves show again.'

"Although she has traditionally been associated with the flirtatious, Miss West has always counted both women and men among her devoted fans.

"'One reason for my success,' she says, 'is that I've never offended women.'"

Mae and Dick Cavett.

Fans loved the rare chance to see Mae on television. One Los Angeles movie theater closed on the night of the broadcast. The marquee read, "CLOSED TONIGHT TO WATCH MAE WEST ON TV."

Critics were not impressed by the special, but seemed to agree on the wonder of "ageless" Mae West.

On April 5, in reviewing the special for the *Los Angeles Times*, Kevin Thomas praised the show with his headline, "What is So Rare as a Mae in April?" Thomas thought that Cavett had saved the best for last – the segment featuring Mae, who had not appeared on television for more than a decade.

"And then there's Mae West," he wrote, "seated on a chaise lounge amidst a few elegant props in an otherwise barren sound stage. Looking very well, Miss West, who has always previously resisted being interviewed on TV, good-naturedly tells Cavett of her battles with censorship, her giving Cary Grant his first leading roles, and, most touchingly, of her admiration for her mother, who always encouraged her but did not live to see her Hollywood stardom.

"Then Mae West appears for a rousing rendition of her special version of "Frankie and Johnny" capped by equally hearty "After You've Gone." Ever the grand entertainer and long an American institution, Mae West makes "Backlot, USA," indeed special!"

The *New York Daily News* proclaimed, "MAE WEST BRINGS SPARK TO CAVETT CATASTROPHE."

And the *New York Times* wrote, "CAVETT'S SPECIAL FLOUNDERS – UNTIL MAE WEST." In his review, John J. O'Connor wrote, "The less said about most of tonight's Dick Cavett special the better. The best segment is saved for last. Cavett goes to visit 'a certain lady of Stage 14.' He asks, 'May I call you Mae?' She responds in that familiar voice promising every earthly delight imaginable. 'Um, yeah, um, of course.' Mae West is peering out from under her blond coiffure again, batting her impossibly long eyelashes before the TV cameras.

"Any reasonable observer might argue that the phenomenon borders on the grotesque. But reason somehow seems puny when confronted with Miss West. She is something – a wonderful, glamorous, talented and marvelously *witty something* – unto herself."

"Where do you do your work?" Cavett asked.

"You, um, mean my thinking?" Mae responded, smiling. She told him she had never learned to type. She wrote longhand in bed.

"Mr. Cavett is also at his best here. He is genuinely interested in his subject. His enthusiasm is infectious."

Mae and Dick Cavett pose on the set of *Dick Cavett's Backlot USA*.

Mae in 1979.

CHAPTER 12

The First Time, and the Last Time

"Poland Spring water comes two ways...
Hmmm... I like that."

IN THE SUMMER OF 1979, Mae West officially became a radio huckster for the first time. The Poland Spring water company approached her to do radio spots advertising their bottled water – a product she had used for years. Poland Spring, located near the town of Lewiston, Maine, was founded in 1845 with the discovery of nearby spring water, originally advertised as having healthy, curative properties. "I'm just crazy about it," she told a reporter for the *Lewiston Evening Journal* on August 21, 1979, "I invited the boys from Poland Spring to come up and seem me sometime, and they did. The rest, as they say, is history." She agreed to make several radio commercials for the company, and said she was "breaking my vow of commercial chastity."

Mae had a belated birthday dinner with reporter Kevin Thomas at her Chinese restaurant of choice in Santa Monica, Madame Wu's Garden. Thomas wrote about their evening for the *Los Angeles Times* on August 29.

Mae with Sylvia Wu at Madame's Wu Garden in Santa Monica.

"I realized that since the '20s, I've been drinking that water," she told Thomas. "I even had it in my dressing room. Never had any other water but Poland Spring for years.

"When I was touring in vaudeville and with my shows I learned that when you drink the water in different cities your stomach gets out of order. Of course, you could drink liquor, but you know me,

I'd never do that. I always had them use Poland Spring for making soup, coffee, all my food. Still do."

In gratitude for so often mentioning their product in the press, the bottled water company had sent cases of water to Mae's apartment through the years. When they asked if she would do commercials, she agreed.

"Once I was on a train to Philadelphia, I think it was," Mae recalled, "when I heard this guy say, 'I hate coming to this town. My fighters always lose.' So I asked him if his guys were drinking the city water. He says, 'Yes,' and I says, 'That's your problem. Get them some Poland Spring water.' Bet they never lost a fight after that.

"Now this friend of mine came up to me, and I was talking about Poland Spring. He says, 'What will people use faucet water for if you get them using Poland Spring for everything?' Well, I says, faucet water's very good for washing cars."

The radio spots were first broadcast in late August, 1979. A subtle jazz piano tinkled in the background.

SPOT #1

ANNOUNCER Ladies and gentlemen, Miss Mae West.

MAE Long before people were drinking Poland Spring water in discotheques because it's in such good taste, I was drinking it in my boudoir 'cause it tastes so good. I've been drinking Poland Spring for over twenty-five years. It's kept me interested longer than any fella. Hmmm… speaking of fellas, Poland Spring is not any Johnny-come-lately. It's been bubbling up from the same cool spring in Maine for close to two hundred years. In fact, they were sending Poland Spring water to the royalty of Europe long before Europe sent its water to us in America. Poland Spring water comes two ways… Hmmm… I like that. With and without bubbles. I also like the big bottle. It's like a good friend.

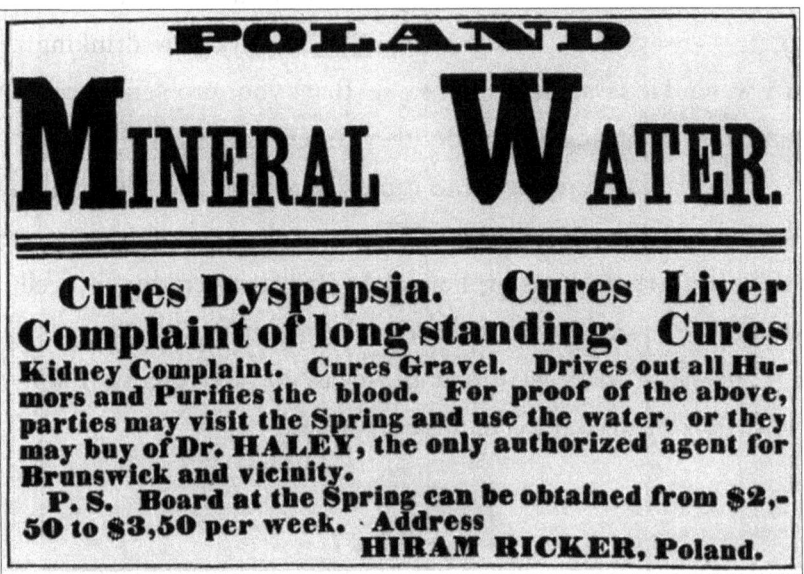

Vintage Poland Spring Mineral Water advertisement.

SPOT #2

ANNOUNCER Ladies and Gentlemen, Miss Mae West

MAE What's all the noise I hear about Poland Spring? I've been drinking Poland Spring water for about… hmmm… twenty years. Started when I was four. I used to have it delivered to my boudoir by a very handsome, young fella. Now he delivers Poland Spring all over the place. Well, I got rid of the fella, but I still keep plenty of Poland Spring around. After all, it comes naturally.

SPOT #3

ANNOUNCER   Ladies and Gentlemen, Mae West

MAE   Let me tell you about this dream I've been having. I'm always very, very hot and very thirsty. Suddenly, a gorgeous fella appears carrying a silver tray and a bottle of Poland Spring water. When I wake up, there's the Poland Spring, but the guy is gone. Hmmm… hmmm… If you're the guy in my dream, why don't you stay around awhile.

SPOT #4

ANNOUNCER   Ladies and Gentlemen, Miss Mae West!

MAE   The boys often ask me how I keep my gorgeous figure. Well, I never smoke and I never drink whiskey. I save myself for bigger things. For the last twenty-five years, I've been sipping nothing but pure, natural Poland Spring water. It's the only thing I've ever been faithful to. Sorry boys. Poland Spring water comes from a quaint little town in Maine. And it's been coming from there a long time. General Grant – one of America's best known drinkers – chased his spirits with it. F.D.R. introduced it to Winnie Churchill. Presidents Garfield, Taft, and Coolidge elected to serve it at the White House. You see, Poland Spring is like me – always in good taste. Hmm…

Poland Spring Water 200th anniversary advertisement.

These national radio commercials were the final scripted broadcast performances of Mae West. The actress spent the following year out of the public eye. She passed away in her apartment at the Ravenswood in Hollywood on November 22, 1980. Mae West was 87 years old.

Mae speaks to students at the University of California, Los Angeles, in 1971.

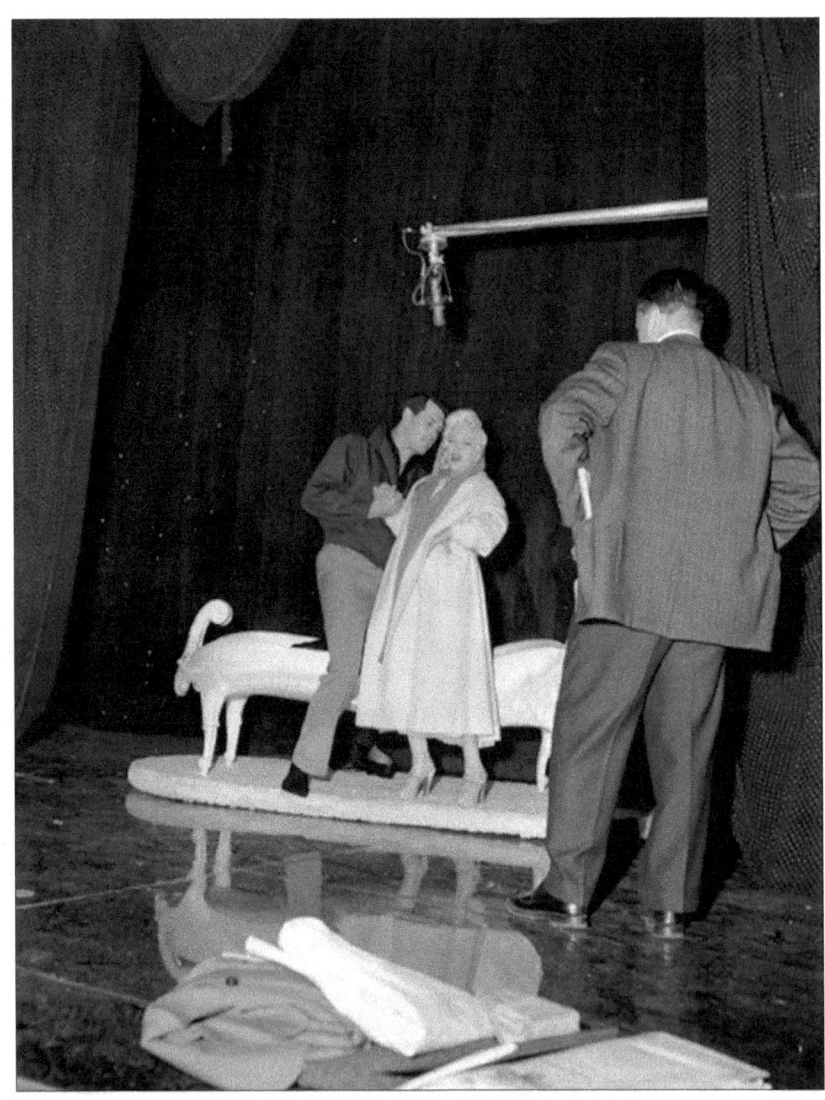

Mae rehearses with Rock Hudson, 1958.

Special Thanks

THANKS TO THE LOS Angeles Public Library and the Beverly Hills Public Library, and the great librarians who work there. Support your local library, an incredible *free* source of reliable news, knowledge, enlightenment, and entertainment. Thanks, too, to the Paley Center for Media in Beverly Hills, and their amazing archive of vintage television broadcasts. And thanks to Alan Young and Connie Hines.

Mae rehearses with Dean Martin and Bob Hope, 1959.

Mae with Red Skelton, 1960.

Bibliography

Chandler, Charlotte. SHE ALWAYS KNEW HOW, MAE WEST A PERSONAL BIOGRAPHY. New York, New York: Simon & Schuster, Inc. 2009

Curry, Ramona. TOO MUCH OF A GOOD THING, MAE WEST AS CULTURAL ICON. Minneapolis, MN: University of Minnesota Press. 1996

Eells, George and Musgrove, Stanley. MAE WEST. New York, New York: William Morrow and Company, Inc. 1982

Hamilton, Marybeth. "WHEN I'M BAD, I'M BETTER." New York, New York: Harper-Collins Publishers, Inc. 1995

Irvin, Richard. FILM STARS' TELEVISION PROJECTS. Jefferson, North Carolina: McFarland & Company. 2017

Kinny, Jack. WALT DISNEY AND ASSORTED OTHER CHARACTERS: AN UNAUTHORIZED ACCOUNT OF THE EARLY YEARS AT DISNEY'S. New York, New York: Harmony Books. 1988

Lamour, Dorothy. MY SIDE OF THE ROAD. Englewood Cliffs, New Jersey: Prentice Hall, Inc. 1980

Leonard, Maurice. MAE WEST, EMPRESS OF SEX. New York, New York: Birch Lane Press. 1992

Louvish, Simon. MAE WEST, IT AIN'T NO SIN. London, England: Faber and Faber. 2005

Mae with Dean Martin.

Michaud, Michael Gregg. MAE WEST SINGS. Los Angeles, CA: Fortunate Rhythm Books. 2017

Tuska, Jon. THE COMPLETE FILMS OF MAE WEST. New York, New York: A Citadel Press Book/Carol Publishing Group. 1973

Ward, Carol M. MAE WEST, A BIO-BIBLIOGRAPHY. Westport, CT: Greenwood Press Inc. 1989

Watts, Jill. MAE WEST, AN ICON IN BLACK AND WHITE. New York, New York: Oxford University Press. 2001

West, Mae. GOODNESS HAD NOTHING TO DO WITH IT. Englewood Cliffs, New Jersey: Prentice Hall, Inc. 1959

Wortis Leider, Emily. BECOMING MAE WEST. New York, New York: Farrar, Straus and Giroux. 1997

Young, Alan. MISTER ED AND ME. New York, New York: St. Martin's Press. 1994

All of the broadcast radio and television programs referenced in this book are available on LP, CD, DVD, and tape, and accessible online.

Alan Young (Wilbur Post), the author, and Connie Hines (Carol Post)

About the Author

MICHAEL GREGG MICHAUD IS the author of the critically acclaimed, best-selling, Lambda Book Award nominated *Sal Mineo, A Biography* (Crown Archetype, 2010). Michaud is the co-author, with actress Diane McBain, of *Famous Enough, A Hollywood Memoir* (Bearmanor Media, 2014), and *Classic Images* 2017 Best Book of the Year and two-time Indie Book Award nominated biography, *Alan Sues, A Funny Man* (BearManor Media, 2016). He is the editor of *Mae West: Between the Covers* (BearManor Media, 2018), writes about Hollywood history, and has contributed to numerous books about show business and the arts. He is also an award-winning poet and photographer. Follow him on Facebook.

www.ingramcontent.com/pod-product-compliance
Lightning Source LLC
Chambersburg PA
CBHW071703160426
43195CB00012B/1556